NELSON

BY

JOHN KNOX LAUGHTON

1895

British Library Cataloguing-in-Publication Data
A catalogue record for this book is available from the
British Library

Horatio Nelson

Horatio Nelson, 1st Viscount Nelson, was a British flag officer in the Royal Navy. He is famed for the part he played in the Napoleonic Wars, most notable amongst his victories being that at the Battle of Trafalgar in 1805.

Born on 29th September 1758 in Norfolk, England, Nelson was the sixth of eleven children born to the Reverend Edmund Nelson and his wife Catherine. His family were well connected; his mother being the grandniece of Robert Walpole (1676-1745), 1st Earl of Oxford, and the *de facto* first Prime Minister of Great Britain, and his godfather, after whom he was named, being 2nd Baron Walpole, of Wolterton, Horatio Walpole (1723-1809). Young Horatio attended Paston Grammar School until the age of 12 when he began his naval career. As an Ordinary Seaman and coxswain, Nelson started his naval career serving under his uncle, Captain Maurice Suckling, on the third-rate HMS Raissonable. Soon after reporting aboard he began his officer training. Unfortunately, Nelson discovered that he was vulnerable to terrible bouts of sea-sickness, a complaint that he was condemned to endure for the rest of his life.

At the age of 20 Nelson was made a captain, going on to serve in the West Indies, the Baltic, and Canada. On his return, with new bride Frances Nesbet, he found himself without command and reduced to half pay. However, following Britain's entrance to the French Revolutionary Wars, in 1793, Nelson found himself in charge of the Agamemnon. During the campaign in the Mediterranean, he lost the sight in his right eye in a battle at Calvi. Not long after, he lost his right arm at the Battle of Santa Cruz de Tenerife.

Nelson was known for being a bold and fearless commander, often to the dismay of his superiors. On one occasion he even defied orders from senior officers to cease action, putting the telescope to his blind eye and claiming he couldn't see their signals. This self-assured attitude did not prevent him from rising through the ranks however. His victories spoke for themselves. One such victory was the triumph of the Battle of the Nile (in 1798) where Nelson destroyed Napoleon's fleet and thus thwarted his ambition to establish a trade route to India.

Although still married, Nelson fell in love with another woman following his posting to Naples. Emma Hamilton, herself married, and Nelson began a lifelong love affair in which they had a daughter together, Horatia, in 1801. In the same year, Nelson was promoted to vice-admiral. He was supremely successful in his position in charge of the British fleet. The Royal Navy won many battles under his command and averted the threat of invasion from the ambitious Napoleon. It was the naval engagement of the Battle of Trafalgar (21st October 1805) that still cements Nelson's place in the history of British warfare however.

This was the most decisive battle of the campaign to stop the French and Spanish Navies, during the War of the Third Coalition (August-December 1805). Aboard the HMS Victory, Nelson led a fleet of 27 ships into battle against 33 enemy vessels just west of Cape Trafalgar, off the coast of Spain. Nelson deviated from conventional naval strategy, dividing his smaller force into two columns directed perpendicularly against the enemy fleet. The tactic worked and the battle was won. However, Nelson was mortally wounded during the engagement, shot by a French sniper.

He was shot in the left shoulder, with the bullet passing through his back.

Despite this injury, as he was being carried below by his men, Nelson asked them to pause while he gave some advice to the midshipman on the handling of the tiller, and then draped a handkerchief over his face to avoid causing alarm amongst the crew. He died on 21st October, 1805. Nelson's body was transported back to England preserved in brandy, and he was subsequently given a state funeral. The first tribute to Nelson was fittingly offered at sea by sailors of Vice-Admiral Dmitry Senyavin's passing Russian squadron, which saluted on learning of the death.

HORATIO NELSON

After the Portrait by J. Hoppner in St. James's Palace

CONTENTS

CHAPTER I

NOTE

THE chief authorities for Nelson's professional life are
Nicolas's *Despatches and Letters of Lord Nelson* (7 vols. 8vo,
1844-6) and James's *Naval History*, checked by ships' logs,
pay-books, etc. etc., the official correspondence of Lord Hood,
Lord St. Vincent, Lord Keith, Sir William Hamilton, and
others, now in the Public Record Office, and by the French
narratives in *Victoires et Conquétes*, etc., Chevalier's *Histoire
de la Marine Française*, and Troude's *Batailles Navales de la
France*. For his private life the principal authority is *The
Hamilton-Nelson Papers* (2 vols. 8vo, 1894), privately printed
for Mr. Alfred Morrison from his splendid collection of
original MSS. Many of these have been used by Mr. J. C.
Jeaffreson in his *Lady Hamilton and Lord Nelson* (2 vols.
post 8vo, 1888) and *The Queen of Naples and Lord Nelson*
(2 vols. post 8vo, 1889). The account of the watering the
fleet at Syracuse and the estimate of Lady Hamilton's public
services here given, follow a discussion of these questions in
The United Service Magazine for April and May 1889. The
ponderous *Life* by Clarke and M'Arthur (2 vols. royal 4to,
1808), which has been the basis of all later Lives, can only
be read with great caution, owing to the easy and uncritical
attitude of the authors. Many of the anecdotes introduced
in it are demonstrably mere galley-yarns, many are certainly incorrectly told, and many rest on very doubtful
authority. But very many of the anecdotes in common
circulation are derived from the *Life* (2 vols. 8vo, 1806) by
Harrison, who wrote it to the order of Lady Hamilton, by
way of magnifying her claims on the Government. It is not
too much to say that the book is "a pack of lies," and that
no one statement in it can be accepted unless it is independently confirmed from other sources.

CHAPTER I

FAMILY AND EARLY SERVICE

In October, 1781, the fortunes of England seemed to have reached their lowest level. War abroad and faction at home had pretty well done their worst for a country ruled by jobbery and corruption. Lord George Germain, branded by a court-martial as "incapable of serving His Majesty in any military capacity," was Secretary for War; and the Earl of Sandwich,

> spared by Fate
> Only to show, on mercy's plan,
> How far and long God bears with man,

was First Lord of the Admiralty. When experienced generals, pitted against each other by the insolence of the one, held divided command with no unity of counsel; when the noblest admirals, feeling neither life nor honour safe under the rule of the other, implored the King to excuse them from service, it is not to be wondered at that the results were big with ruin and dismay. The war against the revolted provinces of North America, assisted by France, Spain, and Holland and supported

B

by the Northern Confederation, seemed as though on
the point of ending in the utter subversion of the
Empire.   The drawn battle on the Doggerbank had
shown us unable to crush even the Dutch; and the
French victory off the mouth of the Chesapeake had
ensured the independence of the colonies.   And as if to
mark the period, Lord Hawke, who twenty years before
had raised our naval power to its greatest height,—
Lord Hawke died on October 17th.

When on the 18th Horace Walpole wrote, "Lord
Hawke is dead, and does not seem to have bequeathed
his mantle to anybody," no one would have been more
surprised than himself had he been told that the mantle
had fallen on a little, insignificant-looking and badly-
dressed cousin of his own; a young captain, for whom
family interest had procured early promotion, but who
was still absolutely unknown, even in the Navy, except
by the few commanding officers who had troubled themselves to think of the abilities of a subordinate.   Many
years, indeed, were still to pass before it was revealed
to the world that Hawke's brightest attributes had
descended to Nelson, and that the pupil of Locker,
Hawke's lieutenant, was to raise the renown of the
British Navy to a still greater height by a victory tran-
scending even that of Quiberon Bay.

Horatio Nelson, fifth son of the Reverend Edmund
Nelson, Rector of Burnham Thorpe in the county of
Norfolk, was born at Burnham Thorpe on September 29th,
1758.   The doctrine of hereditary transmission of genius
seems to find but little support in his pedigree.   On the
father's side he was of a family of parsons.   His grandfather, Edmund Nelson, was Rector of Hilborough in

Norfolk ; his father, also Edmund, was likewise Rector of Hilborough, as well as of Burnham Thorpe, Burnham St. Albert, and Wolterton ; two of his brothers were clergymen, and two of his aunts, his father's sisters, married clergymen ; all, so far as is known, most commonplace men, men who did their duty in their station of life, but without a spark of talent or genius to accredit their relationship.

The mother's side is more promising. Mrs. Nelson's father, also a clergyman, Dr. Maurice Suckling, Prebendary of Westminster and Rector of Wooton in Norfolk, was grandnephew of that Sir John Suckling whose early death may have prevented his reputation as a poet standing higher than it even now does. There had been other men of ability in the family. Robert, Dr. Suckling's grandfather, was Sheriff of Norfolk in 1664 ; Maurice, Dr. Suckling's son, the brother of Mrs. Nelson, served in the navy with some distinction, and when in command of the *Dreadnought* took part in a gallant little action which made some noise at the time.

In October, 1757, Captain Forrest in the *Princess Augusta*, with the *Dreadnought* and *Edinburgh*, all 60-gun ships, was detached by the admiral at Jamaica to cruise off Cape François, in order to intercept the homeward-bound trade on the point of sailing for France. The escort, however, proved stronger than was expected, and on the 21st, a day to be afterwards still more famous in the annals of the Nelson family, it put to sea in advance of the convoy, in order to capture, destroy, or drive off the English cruisers. It consisted of four ships of the line and three large frigates. When Forrest made them out, he summoned his two colleagues, Suckling and Langdon, to a consultation which is said to have lasted just half a minute. As they met on the quarter-deck of the *Princess Augusta*, Forrest said, " Well, gentlemen, you see they are come out to engage us." Suckling replied, " I think it would be a pity to disappoint them " ; Langdon agreed with him, and Forrest closed the conference with, " Very well then ; go on board your ships again." And so forming line, the *Dreadnought* leading, the three ships ran down to attack the seven. A severe action followed, and after about three hours the French drew off, the English not being able to follow. They had twenty-three men killed and about a hundred wounded, many of them danger-ously ; their masts and rigging were cut to pieces ; the *Dreadnought* had lost her main and mizen topmasts ; they were in no state to keep the sea, and were obliged to return to Jamaica. The object of the French com-modore, M. de Kersaint, was really gained, for after he had repaired his damage, his convoy was able to sail without molestation ; but the credit of the action rested with Forrest and his companions, who had not hesitated to attack a very superior force, and had fought it without disadvantage.

Captain Suckling's mother, the wife of Dr. Suckling, was Anne, daughter of Sir Charles Turner, Baronet, of Warham in Norfolk, by Mary, sister of Sir Robert Walpole, K.G., for so many years First Lord of the Treasury, created Earl of Orford in 1742, and of Horatio Walpole, created Lord Walpole of Wolterton in 1756, whose son Horatio, second Lord Walpole of Wolterton, and afterwards Earl of Orford, was godfather and name-father to his little cousin, or, in strictness, his first cousin twice removed. The relationship, though becoming distant, had always been recognised : the family feeling had been kept up ; and it was the Walpoles that, by the presentation of Edmund Nelson to the several rectories of Burnham Thorpe, Burnham St. Albert, and Wolterton, had ensured a provision for Catharine Suckling's husband, as they had probably done before for her father and her brother.

About the name of Horatio there is a little to be said. Sir Edward Walpole, the father of Robert and Horatio, of Mary and another daughter, Dorothy, was the companion in arms during the Civil War of Sir Horatio Townshend, first Viscount Townshend, who was the name-father of Walpole's son Horatio, and the father of Charles, second Viscount Townshend, who married Walpole's daughter Dorothy. The name Horatio, which came into the Nelson family from the Walpoles, came into the Walpole family from the Townshends, to whom it came from the Veres, by the marriage of Sir Roger Townshend (father of Sir Horatio, first Viscount Townshend) with Mary, daughter and heiress of Sir Horatio Vere, Lord Vere of Tilbury, who was knighted by the Earl of Essex at Cadiz in 1596. And thus, though there was no known blood-relationship, Nelson was connected by the rites of the Church and old family friendship with "the fighting Veres," carrying memory back to the sack of Cadiz, and with Sir Roger Townshend, who was knighted by Lord Howard on the quarter-deck of the *Ark* during the battles with the Spanish Armada.

There is another possible, and indeed probable, relationship which would connect the Nelson family still more closely with early naval achievement. They had been settled for many generations in North Norfolk, and must have intermarried with North Norfolk families, and among others with those from which sprang Shovell, Narbrough, Myngs, and Fisher, who were certainly related to most of the minor gentry all round Blakeney. It is no stretch of imagination to suggest that this relationship included the Nelsons; and that the aptitude for naval affairs, the genius for naval command which distinguished Horatio Nelson, was a reversion to the earlier type which first broke through the French line at Barfleur, led Rupert's attack on the Dutch off the North Foreland, or steered the *Margaret and John* into the thick of the Spanish galleons in the battle of Gravelines.

The family of the Rev. Edmund Nelson was a large one. It numbered eleven in all, boys and girls; but of these, three died in infancy, and four others before Horatio, three of them unmarried, the fourth married but leaving no child. Three were still alive at the time of Horatio's death: William, seventeen months older than himself, the companion of his infancy and of his school-days, his friend and correspondent through life, a clergyman, Prebendary and Vice-Dean of Canterbury, created Earl Nelson of Trafalgar after his brother's death; Susanna, born in 1755, who married in 1780 Mr. Thomas Bolton, to whose son the title passed on the failure of William's male descendants; and Catherine, born in 1767, who in 1787 married Mr. George Matcham and had issue. Mrs. Nelson died in December 1767, a few months after Catherine's birth, her eldest living son, Maurice, being then a little over fourteen, and Horatio just nine.

Of Nelson's childhood we really know very little.
He himself has chronicled that he was at the grammar-
school at Norwich, and afterwards at North Walsham,
where a brick in the wall is still pointed out, marked
with the letters H. N.   Many years later Captain
George Manby wrote that he had been Nelson's school-
fellow at Downham ; but the recollections of an old man
are not always to be trusted, and in any case, as Nelson
himself did not remember it, it must have been for a
very short time and in his infancy.   It appears certain
that North Walsham was his last school, and probable
that he went to it in the January after his mother's
death.   As to the many anecdotes of his childhood, they
have either been made to order, or are exaggerations of
old family jokes.   That he told his grandmother he had
seen nothing to be afraid of, and that his grandmother
repeated it as something grand ; that he stole the pears
out of his schoolmaster's garden, and jeered at his school-
fellows for not venturing, and such like, may be true
enough, without being worth repeating : many a little
fellow has said or done the same, and many a grandmother has asserted her belief that there never was
such a boy.   We approach the domain of known fact
when, on November 17th, 1770, Captain Suckling was
appointed to the command of the 64-gun ship *Raisonnable*,
and on January 1st, 1771, entered his little nephew on
her books as a midshipman.

Just then there was some excitement in the Navy,
which had been in a state of dull quietude for the last
seven years, since the Peace of Paris.   The action of
Spain in June, 1770, forcibly seizing the Falkland Islands
and ejecting the English garrison, had disturbed this

repose. The *Civis Romanus* theory was in the air. Spain
was to be taught that she could not be allowed to settle
international questions in this arbitrary manner where
England was concerned. Many ships were put in commission, and no doubt, on joining the *Raisonnable* at
Chatham, the young midshipman heard a good deal about
bringing "the haughty Dons" to reason. The haughty
Dons were, however, sufficiently reasonable to understand
that they had provoked a storm which they could not
stand against unaided. France, whatever might be her
goodwill, was not then prepared to support her with arms,
and so Spain withdrew her pretensions and her troops.
The English soldiers returned to Port Egmont, and the
matter happily ended with the paying off of several of
the ships which had been specially commissioned. Suckling was turned over to the *Triumph*, the guardship in
the Medway, and took his nephew with him, this time
in the rating of " captain's servant."

At that date there were two officially recognised ways
for a young gentleman to join the Navy. One was as a
midshipman from the Royal Academy at Portsmouth,
after a two years' course of study; the other, and more
usual, was as captain's servant, which did not and was
not understood to convey any idea of menial duties,
but simply of dependence. Nothing was more common
than for the captain's son or brother, cousin or, as in
this case, nephew, to be also the captain's servant; and
as with his own relations, so also was it with those of his
friends. The custom was as old as any organisation in
the Navy; but towards the end of Queen Elizabeth's
reign, when it was found that the privilege was abused,
and that captains entered servants in excessive numbers,

a limit was fixed at two for every fifty or part of fifty in the ship's company; and so it continued, with scarcely a break, for two hundred years. It did, of course, bring into the service many officers of the best class; but it also added largely to the emoluments of the captain, who received the pay of his servants, their necessary expenses being provided for by an allowance from their friends. In a similar way, other officers were allowed to enter their own servant,—that is, to bring a young relation into the service, and have him trained, according to the custom of the time, as a "naval cadet." In a court-martial held in 1777, it was incidentally stated that the master's servant was doing duty as a quarter-deck petty officer,— that is, as a midshipman—and that the young man was the master's brother.

Besides these, the officially prescribed ways for a young gentleman to enter the Navy, a large number entered in some other irregular rating, as "able seaman" or midshipman. An able seaman was supposed to be, as the name implies, qualified to perform a seaman's duty; a midshipman was supposed to be a capable petty officer; and to enter a little boy, fresh from school or perhaps from the nursery, in either rating was an abuse which was not dishonest only because it was universal, and was known by the Admiralty to be so. Suckling's rating his twelve-year-old nephew as a midshipman in the *Raisonnable* was such an abuse; his rating him captain's servant in the *Triumph* was in strict accordance with the Instructions. What was not in accordance with the Instructions was the forthwith sending him out of the ship, lending him to a merchant-ship, while borne on the books of the *Triumph* for pay and victuals.

But this again was sanctioned by custom. Every admiral and captain in the service did it, and knew that it was done, and believed that there was no harm in it. It was not till seventeen years later that, in 1788, a check was put on the practice by the celebrated court-martial on Captain Coffin, who was tried on a charge of knowingly signing a false muster-book, four young gentlemen, borne as captain's servants, being therein declared to be present, when in fact they had never been on board the ship.

Clearly such a case, and it was the common type, was morally as well as legally wrong. For a very little boy to be learning his letters or even his Latin Grammar on shore while he, or rather his captain for him, was receiving pay and victuals as an apprentice on board ship, was clearly as contrary to the spirit as to the letter of the law. Suckling could at least have shown that his servant was learning the rudiments of seamanship in a rough but practical way. The ship to which Horatio Nelson was lent was commanded by John Rathbone, who had served through a great part of the Seven Years' War as a master's mate of the *Dreadnought*, and had passed his examination; but on being paid off, and finding neither promotion nor even employment in the Navy, had returned to the merchants' service, and was now master of a ship trading to the West Indies.

The voyage out and home would seem to have lasted about a year, and in July, 1772, the boy returned to the *Triumph*. The exact date, of which there is no record, was probably the 19th, when he was rated midshipman. He was now, he says, a practical seaman. No doubt he had picked up a good deal, including the swagger. "Aft

the most honour, forward the better man," he had learned
to say, and to fancy himself all "heart of yarn and
Stockholm tar." Suckling easily knocked this nonsense
out of him ; and yet it is possible that the consciousness
of having once felt it remained, and gave him through
life a sense of kinship with the fore-mast men and a
marvellous power of winning their love and confidence.
Meantime he was set to study navigation, and as a
reward of industry was allowed to go in the decked
long-boat, the *Triumph's* tender in fact ; and so gradually, he says, he became a good pilot for vessels of
that description in the Medway and the Thames, and
confident of himself among rocks and sands.

In the spring of 1773, at his own earnest request,
supported, no doubt, by Suckling's, Captain Lutwidge
entered him as a midshipman on board the *Carcass*, then
fitting for a voyage of Arctic discovery in company with
the *Racehorse*, commanded by Captain Phipps afterwards
Lord Mulgrave. The share of a boy not yet fifteen
in such an expedition was of course very small ; it is
notable only as a part of the education which was
forming the man ; an education of trial and hardship, of
seamanship and ready expedients. On their return, the
ships paid off at Deptford on October 14th, 1773 ; and
on the 27th, young Nelson, who had meantime been
borne on the books of the *Triumph*, was rated as a midshipman of the *Seahorse*, a 24-gun frigate, being described
on her books as "aged 18" ; it was a way then in vogue,
which often served to cloak gross irregularities.

The *Seahorse* was at this time fitting out for the East
Indies, one of the squadron which sailed on November
19th, 1773, under the command of Commodore Sir

Edward Hughes, the same who afterwards fought five indecisive battles with M. de Suffren, in which pluck and goodwill held their own against superior science and disaffection. It is impossible to doubt that as the news of these actions reached him, Nelson, if only from his personal interest in Hughes, closely studied the details, and marked where Hughes, where Suffren had the advantage, and how tactical skill on the one side, or unity of purpose on the other, was singly insufficient. But this was nearly ten years later.

The captain of the *Seahorse* was George Farmer, who afterwards, on October 6th, 1779, commanded the *Quebec* in an unequal action against the French frigate *Surveillante*. The *Quebec* caught fire and blew up, with the loss of most of her men. Farmer, who had been already wounded in the arm, was last seen sitting on the cathead encouraging his men. In recognition of his bravery and good conduct, his eldest son, then a lad of seventeen who had been a captain's servant in the *Seahorse*, was made a baronet, and a pension of £200 a year was conferred on the widow, with an additional £25 for each of her nine children; in order (in the very exceptional words of the Admiralty minute) "to excite an emulation in other officers to distinguish themselves in the same manner, and render Captain Farmer's fate rather to be envied than pitied, as it would give them reason to hope that if they should lose their lives with the same degree of stubborn gallantry, it would appear to posterity that their services had met with the approbation of their sovereign." Such was the captain under whose care and discipline Nelson was placed as he was changing from a boy into a young man. He was fortunate too in his companions, with one of whom, Thomas Troubridge, a year or two older than himself, his later associations were peculiarly intimate.

On April 5th, 1774, Nelson was rated an "able seaman," and on October 31st, 1775, was again rated midshipman. It is not to be supposed that these changes made any real change to the boy, further than the trifling difference of pay, between three and four pounds a year. The number of midshipmen on board the frigate was limited, and the first change meant that, for some reason or other, Captain Farmer wished to give the rating to some one else, to his own son, in fact, the future baronet; when there was again a vacancy, it was given to Nelson. How little real difference there was appears from Nelson's own statement, that when he first joined the *Seahorse*, as a midshipman, "he watched in the fore-top," and in time, when an able seaman, "was placed on the quarterdeck." In the *Seahorse* he "visited almost every part of the East Indies, from Bengal to Bussorah"; but under the trying climate, possibly of the Persian Gulf, his health gave way, and on March 14th, 1776, the commodore ordered him to be discharged to the *Dolphin* for a passage to England. The kindness of Captain Pigot, he says, saved his life, and he seems to have regained his health by the time the *Dolphin* reached England. She was paid off on September 24th, 1776; and two days after Nelson was appointed lieutenant of the 64-gun ship *Worcester*, by acting order from Sir James Douglas, the Commander-in-Chief at Portsmouth. Captain Suckling was at this time Comptroller of the Navy, and the interest of the Comptroller was, in some respects, as great as, if not greater than, that of the First Lord of the Admiralty.

Nelson joined the *Worcester* on October 8th, and was kindly received by her captain, Mark Robinson, to whom he brought a letter of introduction from his uncle. Robinson took him to call on the Commander-in-Chief, and for the short time they remained at Portsmouth treated him rather as an equal and a friend than as a very young acting-lieutenant. He was a good and brave officer, and five years later, in command of the *Shrewsbury*, led the van in the unfortunate action off the mouth of the Chesapeake, where, by the loss of his leg and the severe damage sustained not only by the *Shrewsbury* but by all the ships in the van, he impressed a valuable lesson on Nelson's tactical studies. During the winter the *Worcester* was sent to Gibraltar in charge of convoy, and Nelson was gratified by being placed in charge of a watch, and by Robinson's compliment that "he felt as easy when he, Nelson, was on deck as any officer in the ship." On their return to England he passed his examination at the Navy Office, and the next day, April 10th, 1777, was promoted to be lieutenant of the *Lowestoft*, a 32-gun frigate fitting for the Jamaica station.

When Nelson joined this ship with his first commission, he received from his uncle, the Comptroller, a very remarkable letter on his duties as an officer; remarkable, as showing the low standard of order, when an experienced captain thought it necessary to point out and insist on matters of detail which have long seemed commonplaces of the service, such, for instance, as to see the yards square, the ropes taut, no ropes hanging over the side, and to be particular in working the sails together; "Nothing," he wrote, "is so lubberly as to hoist one sail after another." The captain of the *Lowe-stoft* was William Locker, who had distinguished himself in the Seven Years' War, when first-lieutenant of the *Experiment*, by boarding and capturing the French *Télémaque*. He had afterwards, in the *Sapphire* frigate, been a witness of the battle of Quiberon Bay, and in March, 1760, had joined the *Royal George*, Hawke's flagship in the Bay of Biscay. Hawke took much kindly notice of Locker, who has left us a most favourable opinion, not of the great admiral's achievements, which are written in the history of Europe, but of his discipline and of his good influence on his own officers and on the Navy generally. Locker always regarded this as the happiest time of his service: "He was received into the personal friendship of his admiral, and, profiting by his advice and experience, he matured much of that professional knowledge which he had previously gained."

What Locker had received from Hawke he now passed on to Nelson. It would be too much to say that he foresaw the importance of his lessons; it is enough to suppose that, himself a good officer filled with anecdotes of the service and illustrations of former wars, within his own experience or handed down by tradition, he found in his young lieutenant, recommended to him in the first instance as the nephew of the Comptroller, a thirst for knowledge, a zeal for the service, a restless energy, which won on his heart and led him to treat his junior with an affectionate freedom unusual even now, but still more so in 1777. The great debt which Nelson owed to Locker, and through Locker to Hawke, has perhaps not been sufficiently recognised; for indeed it can only be recognised by considering what sort of a man Locker was, a man who not only had been taken by the hand by Hawke, but who had made it the business of his leisure to collect a vast store of information respecting the service, a store which was afterwards the basis of Charnock's *Biographia Navalis*.

Of Nelson's service in the *Lowestoft* there is little to say. He himself has related one incident which is notable, not so much for itself as for the way in which he introduced the story and told it. In the last year of the century he was asked by M'Arthur, one of the editors of the *Naval Chronicle*, to furnish some notes of his life for the use of that periodical, and contributed a sketch, in the course of which, after speaking of his joining the *Lowestoft*, he went on: "Whilst in this frigate, an event happened which presaged my character; and as it conveys no dishonour to the officer alluded to, I shall relate it. Blowing a gale of wind and very heavy sea, the frigate captured an American letter of marque. The first-lieutenant was ordered to board her, which he did not do owing to the very high sea. On his return on board, the captain said, 'Have I no officer in the ship who can board the prize?' On which the master ran to the gangway to get into the boat; when I stopped him, saying, 'It is my turn now; and if I come back, it is yours.' This little incident has often occurred to my mind; and I know it is my disposition that difficulties and dangers do but increase my desire of attempting them."

What others may think of at least equal importance is his statement that, finding the frigate not sufficiently active for his mind, he got sent into a schooner, the *Lowestoft's* tender, and in her made himself "a complete

pilot for all the passages through the islands situated on
the north side of Hispaniola." His later service did not
indeed take him to those waters; but familiarity with
ticklish navigation in one sea is the best teacher for
similar work in others; and the youthful practice on
the north coast of Hispaniola prepared the man for bold
navigation in Aboukir Bay, in the Sound, or in the Lion's
Gulf.

Early in 1778 Sir Peter Parker, at that time Commander-in-Chief at Jamaica, moved Nelson into the
Bristol, his flagship, then considered as in itself a promotion. It was, at any rate, a certain road to it,
especially on a sickly station like Port Royal. At that
time all vacancies occurring on any foreign station were
filled up by the Commander-in-Chief, and such promotions
were generally confirmed by the Admiralty, or, indeed,
always when the vacancies were caused by death.
When the vacancy to be filled up was a commander's,
the admiral, as a rule, promoted his first-lieutenant; if
it was a lieutenant's, he promoted the senior mate of the
flagship. He kept a list of men whom, for family or
other reasons, he wished to promote, and as occasion
offered appointed them to the flagship in turn, each
one as the junior of his rank, and moving gradually up
till he became first and was in turn promoted. With
such an appointment merit might occasionally have
something to do, but as a rule it depended entirely on
interest. Parker's quickness to discover the ability of
the young lieutenant of the *Lowestoft* has often been
spoken of. There had been no way in which Nelson
could possibly have shown any; and though Locker may
have been asked for his opinion of the lad (he was but

little, over nineteen), there can be no doubt that his chief merit in Parker's eyes was his relationship to the Comptroller.

In the present age of liberty, equality, and competitive examinations, it is difficult to realise that through last century, and indeed down to the middle of this, and even later, interest was almost everything; and that an admiral was more likely to promote his own kinsman, or the kinsman of a friend, or of some one who might, he judged, be able and willing to render him some equivalent service, than a mere nobody, however good an officer he had shown himself. There were indeed exceptions. During the great war Lord St. Vincent and, taught by him and his own sense of right, Nelson made many promotions dependent on merit and good service; but such conduct was even then exceptional, and would have been still more so five-and-twenty years earlier. Every one will admit that good service in time of war ought to be a paramount claim to promotion : even those who were the most notorious jobbers would have admitted it theoretically, though in practice they put it far from them; but failing a demand in favour of merit, which in time of peace does not always display itself very clearly, promotion by interest was, in some respects, not so bad for the service as it appears at first sight. For one thing, it promoted a considerable number of men at an early age, and there was always a possibility that among these there might be some man of ability and genius who would come to the front when wanted.

When promotion from the rank of lieutenant is regulated almost entirely by seniority, it is rare for a man to be made a commander before he is thirty-five; more commonly he is verging on forty. With from five to ten years as commander, and fifteen or sixteen as captain, the defence which has been adopted against filling the admiral's list with old men is to retire all captains at the age of fifty-five; but for many of those who do become admirals it is a mere chance between promotion and retirement. Few indeed are younger than fifty. But during the greater part of last century, when lieutenants were frequently made at the age of eighteen and became captains before they were twenty, even though further promotion was delayed, they were still comparatively young when they got their flag. Boscawen was a rear-admiral and on his way out to India as Commander-in-Chief when he was thirty-seven. Hawke, who was not the son of a peer, was forty-two when he was sent out in command of the Channel Fleet and annihilated L'Étenduère in the Bay of Biscay. Howe and Jervis, of a later date, were involved in the stagnation of the list which followed the War of the Austrian Succession, and were respectively forty-four and fifty-two when they got their flag; but Howe was a captain at twenty, and even Jervis was one at twenty-five. Later on, again, promotion was accelerated, and Nelson became a rear-admiral when a little over thirty-eight; under the present system he would have been but a young captain, if not still a commander, at the time of his death.

His probation in the *Bristol* was not long. On December 8th, 1778, when about six weeks over twenty, he was promoted to be commander of the *Badger* brig, from which, after six months of uneventful cruising, he was further promoted on June 11th, 1779, to be captain

of the *Hinchinbroke*, a frigate-built French prize which
had been brought into the service, and so named in compliment to the Earl of Sandwich. She was just then out
on a cruise, and as she overstayed her time, much anxiety
was felt about her at Jamaica. It was reported that she
was captured; and when D'Estaing, after his ignomini-
ous repulse by Barrington at St. Lucia, his inglorious
success at Grenada, and his discreditable retreat from
St. Kitts, came to the Cape, where there were said to be
upwards of twenty thousand men ready to embark and
a large number of transports collected to receive them,
people supposed that he might prove more enterprising
against a defenceless colony than he had shown himself
against a line of battle. Every possible preparation
was made in Jamaica for his coming. The few ships
were moored in commanding positions; all those in the
neighbourhood were called in; batteries were thrown up
on shore, and some seven thousand men were got together, five hundred of them in Fort Charles, under
Nelson's command. It was a false alarm, false from
beginning to end. The rumoured fleet of transports at
the Cape was merely the homeward trade for France
waiting for a convoy. There was no such body of
troops; and D'Estaing, though under orders to return
with the trade, yielded to the prayers of the revolted
colonists and sailed for the coast of North America, in
order to meet with another repulse at Savannah, after
which he went back to France.

Meantime the *Hinchinbroke* got safely to Jamaica, and
Nelson, having joined her, was presently ordered on a
cruise for a couple of months. He came in again in
the middle of September, having made four prizes which

he calculated would bring him about £800. At Port
Royal he lived on shore with Captain Cornwallis, with
whom he contracted a lifelong friendship. The fortune
of the service did not bring them much together afterwards; but at a very critical moment in their careers,
and in the history of the country, the two men were
supplementing each other's work, the one commanding
the blockade of Brest, the other of Toulon.

At this time Nelson was offered the command of a
large Spanish store-ship, which had been brought in
by Captain Inglis of the *Salisbury*, and was now ordered
to be fitted as a 36-gun frigate. He declined her,
possibly because in the *Hinchinbroke* he was appointed to
the naval command of an expedition against the city of
Granada on Lake Nicaragua. Unfortunately the season
was too late by three months. Instead of arriving at
San Juan in January, when the floods had subsided and
the weather was fine, they did not arrive till the middle
of April, when the rainy season had set in. The result
was that the men, wet through two or three times a
day, and exposed by night to pestilential damp and
malaria, fell sick rapidly. The seamen seem to have
suffered most. Their work was extremely heavy.
Nelson claimed to have carried troops in boats up a
river which none but Spaniards had ascended since the
time of the buccaneers; to have boarded, so to speak,
an outpost of the enemy situated on an island in the
river; to have made batteries and afterwards fought
them; and to have been a principal cause of the success;
and his statement is fully corroborated by the official
report of Colonel Polson, who commanded the troops.
" I want words," he wrote, "to express the obligations I

owe Captain Nelson. He was the first on every service, whether by night or by day. There was scarcely a gun but what was pointed by him or Lieutenant Despard."

Nelson's energy and zeal long supported him, but at last he too was prostrated by the prevailing fever and dysentery. He was apparently in a dying condition when he was recalled to Jamaica by his appointment to the 44-gun ship *Janus*, and took a passage in the *Victor* sloop. He was succeeded in the *Hinchinbroke* by his friend Cuthbert Collingwood, who, though some ten years older, was only now promoted to the rank of captain. It gives a clearer idea of the virulence of the sickness to find that out of a complement of two hundred men the *Hinchinbroke* buried one hundred and forty-five; and Nelson believed that forty-five more died shortly afterwards. At Jamaica he himself lay for some time at death's door, his life being probably preserved by the tender care and indefatigable nursing of Lady Parker. He was still unable to undertake any duty, and on September 4th sailed for England in the *Lion*, with his friend Cornwallis. He landed at Portsmouth on November 24th, 1780, and went straight to Bath, the refuge of invalid naval officers all through last century. He was then so ill that he had to be carried to and from bed, in the most excruciating pain.

By the middle of January he wrote that, being physicked three times a day, drinking the waters three times, and bathing every other night, he was on the mending hand; and on the 28th he began to speak of being appointed to a ship. He had not yet, he said, quite recovered the use of his limbs, but had no doubt he would be perfectly well in two or three weeks. He was, however, still in the doctor's hands through February ; but by Monday, March 5th, he wrote : " I never was so well in health that I can remember. I have fixed to come to town on Wednesday or Thursday next," a fixture afterwards postponed till the following Monday. It was at this time that he had occasion to remark on the smallness of the fees charged by his physician, Doctor Woodward, and wished to increase the payment, to which Woodward replied : " Pray, Captain Nelson, allow me to follow what I consider to be my professional duty. Your illness, sir, has been brought on by serving your king and country, and, believe me, I love both too well to be able to receive any more."

The Bath cure did not, however, prove quite so well established as Nelson had thought, and through May he was again under the doctor's hands in London, where he was living with his uncle William Suckling, of the Custom-House, the Comptroller to whom he owed so much having died three years before, in July, 1778. On May 7th he wrote to his brother William : " I have entirely lost the use of my left arm, and very near of my left leg and thigh, and am at present under the care of a Mr. Adair, an eminent surgeon in London ; but he gives me hopes a few weeks will remove my disorder, when I will certainly come into Norfolk, and spend my time there till I am employed." And this he seems to have done.

CHAPTER II

In August, 1781, Captain Nelson was appointed to command the *Albemarle*, a 28-gun frigate, which he commissioned at Woolwich on the 24th. Like all of her class she had very poor accommodation. Nelson, however, wrote that he was "perfectly satisfied with her. She has a bold entrance and a clean run"; and again some months later: "She has some good sailing in her. The *Argo*, a new 44, we can spare a good deal of sail, and I think we go full as well as the *Enterprise*." But it was a marked feature of Nelson's genius to "think all his geese swans," and to believe his ship, as afterwards his fleet, the very best in the Navy. So also as to his officers and ship's company. In the *Albemarle* he found his "quarter-deck filled with very gentlemanly young men and seamen, an exceeding good master, and good warrant officers." A little later he wrote: "I have an exceeding good ship's company. Not a man or officer in her I would wish to change!" Then the ship's company were "as good a set of men as ever he saw"; Mitchell, a mate, was "an exceeding good petty officer"; Bromwich, a lieutenant, was a "very good officer"; the master was "the best master he ever saw since he went to sea." It was needless to say he was happy in his ship's company, and "no one could be happier in their officers than he was." This was the first time, but the same or similar expressions were continually repeated through his whole service.

It is not necessary to suppose that Nelson was exceptionally fortunate in his officers and men. It is, on the contrary, a curious thing that only one officer of his training, Sir William Hoste, proved himself an exceptional man; Sir Edward Berry and Sir Thomas Hardy were good men, but not better than dozens of their compeers. Apart from Nelson, most were of a very ordinary type. With Nelson they were inspired, not by any care or pretence on his part, but by his genuine nature. Whatever was his was the best. The effect of this was that any officer or man coming under his command presently felt that his chief considered him one of the finest fellows that ever lived, and forthwith endeavoured, so far as lay in his power, to show that this flattering opinion was a true one.

Although in war time, the *Albemarle's* service was in no respect brilliant. A trip to Elsinore in charge of convoy gave Nelson some experience of northern navigation, which was to bear fruit in due time. In the spring of 1782 he was at Portsmouth and Cork, waiting for a convoy to the St. Lawrence, with which he sailed in the end of April, in company with Captain Pringle in the *Dædalus*, going on the Newfoundland station. In the end of May he arrived at St. John's, and there heard news of the battle of April 12th. After taking the convoy up the river he sailed on a cruise, from which, after an absence of ten weeks, he returned to Quebec in the middle of September, "knocked up with scurvy, having for eight weeks," he wrote, "myself and all the officers, lived upon salt beef; nor had the ship's company had a fresh meal since April 7th."

The Navy had not then learned how to avoid this direful pest, but Nelson shows that he already understood the importance of fresh beef. Of that, and of the measures which during his long blockade of Brest Hawke had taken to ensure a full supply, we need not doubt he had heard from Locker; and we may be sure that Locker's teaching, now brought home to him by his own experience, was never afterwards forgotten. This was the real fruit of the cruise, more valuable a thousand times than the prizes which were taken but did not come in; more valuable than even his escape from the squadron of four French ships of the line which chased him in Boston Bay.

After a few weeks at Quebec, where the health of the ship's company was re-established, the *Albemarle* went to New York, and Nelson made the acquaintance of Lord Hood, who had just been made an Irish peer for his services on April 12th. Hood seems to have at once conceived a high opinion of the young captain of the *Albemarle*, and with the consent of Rear-Admiral Digby, the Commander-in-Chief in North America, agreed to take him with him to the West Indies. It was at this time, too, that Nelson was introduced to Prince William Henry, afterwards Duke of Clarence and King William the Fourth, who many years later said: "I was then a midshipman on board the *Barfleur*, lying in the Narrows off Staten Island, and had the watch on deck, when Captain Nelson, of the *Albemarle*, came in his barge

alongside, who appeared to be the merest boy of a captain
I ever beheld ; and his dress was worthy of attention.
He had on a full-laced uniform ; his lank, unpowdered
hair was tied in a stiff Hessian tail, of an extraordinary
length ; the old-fashioned flaps of his waistcoat added
to the general quaintness of his figure, and produced an
appearance which particularly attracted my notice ; for
I had never seen anything like it before, nor could I
imagine who he was, nor what he came about. My
doubts were, however, removed when Lord Hood introduced me to him. There was something irresistibly
pleasing in his address and conversation ; and an enthusiasm when speaking on professional subjects that
showed he was no common being. Nelson after this
went with us to the West Indies, and served under
Lord Hood's flag during his indefatigable cruise off Cape
François. Throughout the whole of the American War
the height of Nelson's ambition was to command a line-
of-battle ship ; as for prize-money, it never entered his
thoughts : he had always in view the character of his
maternal uncle."

Nelson himself, writing to Captain Locker from the
West Indies on February 25th, 1783, said : "My situation in Lord Hood's fleet must be in the highest degree
flattering to any young man. He treats me as if I was
his son, and will, I am convinced, give me anything I
can ask of him ; nor is my situation with Prince William
less flattering. Lord Hood was so kind as to tell him
(indeed, I cannot make use of expressions strong enough
to describe what I felt) that if he wished to ask questions
relative to naval tactics, I could give him as much information as any officer in the fleet. He will be, I am

certain, an ornament to our service. He is a seaman,
which you could hardly suppose. Every other qualifica-
tion you may expect from him." As at this time Nelson
had never served with a fleet, his knowledge of fleet
manœuvring and naval tactics must have been entirely
theoretical; and it is difficult to see where he could
have picked it up except in conversation with Locker,
with Cornwallis, possibly with Parker, who might serve
as the horrid example, and more recently with Hood.

His coming to the West Indies, however, led to no
results. The war was practically over; and except a
casual and unsuccessful attempt in March, 1783, to retake
Turk's Island, nothing occurred worthy of notice. In
May the fleet was ordered home, and the *Albemarle*,
being sent on in advance, arrived at Spithead on June
25th, 1783. She was paid off on July 3rd, and Nelson
was placed on half-pay.

On coming to London, he was busy for some time
"attempting," he wrote, "to get the wages due to my
good fellows for various ships they have served in in
the war. The disgust of the seamen to the Navy is all
owing to the infernal plan of turning them over from
ship to ship, so that men cannot be attached to their
officers, or the officers care twopence about them." This
is only an early instance of the constant care Nelson
took of the interests of those under his command. They
were as part of his family, and throughout his whole career
to have served with him was a certain claim to his good
offices; lieutenant, master, or seaman, he interested himself in all. This was no mere selfish policy; it was a
true sentiment of the brotherhood of arms. But no policy
could have been more successful; as he loved his officers

and men, they loved him, and the feeling spread till it extended through the Navy. On paying off the *Albemarle*, he wrote : " The whole ship's company offered, if I could get a ship, to enter for her immediately ; but I have no thought of going to sea, for I cannot afford to live on board ship in such a manner as is going on at present."

And so in October, after a short visit to Burnham, he applied for leave of absence, and went over to France ; intending, it would appear, to stay abroad for some time. He took up his residence at St. Omer, and while studying French, fell in love with a Miss Andrews, a daughter of an English clergyman there. In January, 1784, he consulted his uncle, William Suckling, who consented to allow him £100 a year so as to enable him to marry ; and on the strength of that increase to his income, he seems to have proposed to Miss Andrews and to have been refused. It was not a thing that he was likely to talk about ; but his letter to Suckling is dated January 14th, 1784, and on the 19th he was in London. That something had happened to make him desirous of occupation is clear ; for notwithstanding his previous resolve, he was on March 19th appointed to the *Boreas*, a 28-gun frigate, superseding Captain Thomas Wells who had commissioned her five or six months before. She was under orders for the Leeward Islands ; but it was the middle of May before she sailed from Spithead, Lady Hughes, the wife of the Commander-in-Chief, and her daughter taking a passage in her, and Nelson's brother William going as her chaplain.

Of William Nelson in this capacity a very few words will be sufficient. He had previously wished to join the

Albemarle, but as his brother threw cold water on the idea, he gave it up for the time.   Now, the opportunity of seeing the West Indies revived it, and though Nelson did not approve of his entering the Navy, or think he would like it, he consented to his coming.   William Nelson, however, soon found that his health could not stand the climate, which might easily be disagreeable to a man of a full habit of body and self-indulgent temperament, as he was ; and within a few weeks of the *Boreas* arriving on the station, he left her and returned to England.

For Lady Hughes Nelson conceived a strong dislike. From the beginning he thought he was imposed on in being asked to take her and her family out.   " I shall not be sorry to part with them," he wrote from Madeira ; "they are pleasant people, but an incredible expense." By the time he arrived at Antigua he seems to have been heartily tired of them, more especially of Lady Hughes, whom he curtly described as having " an eternal clack."   Of the Admiral too he presently formed an unfavourable opinion.   Sir Richard Hughes was a brave, amiable, and easy-tempered man, but not by any means an ideal commander-in-chief.   " I do not like him," Nelson wrote, within a very few weeks after he joined the flag; " he bows and scrapes too much for me."   And later on : "The Admiral lives in a boarding-house at Barbadoes, not much in the style of a British Admiral " ; and again : "Sir Richard Hughes is a fiddler ; therefore, as his time is taken up tuning that instrument, the squadron is cursedly out of tune."   This, however, was after, or perhaps in consequence of, a serious difference of opinion with the Admiral on two points of service, and a disobedience of his orders which marked an extraordinary resolution in so young an officer.

The first of these was a question arising out of the Navigation Laws, which, it will be remembered, placed great restrictions on foreign ships trading with British colonies. The people of the United States had become foreigners, but wished to retain the commercial privileges which they had enjoyed while they were British subjects. In this the island merchants were at one with them. The trade with the States was lucrative; they had no wish that it should be put a stop to, and approached the Admiral with a request to sanction it. Hughes, with easy-going carelessness, had tacitly agreed; but when Nelson and Collingwood (now in command of the *Mediator*) called his attention to the Navigation Act, he gave them orders to carry it into effect. Accordingly, when Nelson went to St. Kitts as senior officer, he turned away all the American ships; on which the colonial merchants again memorialised the Admiral, with such success that he sent Nelson an order not to hinder American ships from coming or going, if the governors of the islands chose to allow them.

The Governor of St. Kitts did choose to allow them, and on Nelson remonstrating with him, said that "old generals were not in the habit of taking advice from young gentlemen"; to which Nelson replied, "I have the honour, sir, of being as old as the Prime Minister of England, and think myself as capable of commanding one of His Majesty's ships as that minister is of governing the State." His reply to Hughes was a more serious matter; it was in effect that the order was contrary to the Act of Parliament, and he should decline obeying it.

Hughes, easy-tempered as he was, was very angry, and wished to supersede Nelson; but, on talking the matter over with the flag-captain, found that the general opinion in the squadron was that Nelson was right, that the order was illegal, and that they would not be bound to obey it. It accordingly became a dead-letter; but it was not rescinded; nor did the Admiral give Nelson any support against the attacks of the infuriated colonists.

He had seized five American ships, confining their masters on board; and while the question of the ships was under adjudication, actions for illegal detention of the men were brought against him, and damages laid at £4000. The ships were condemned; but Nelson remained a prisoner on board his own ship, subject to arrest if he was found on shore, and in the certainty that if tried he would be cast in the whole sum. Mr. Herbert, the President of Nevis, offered to be bail for him to the amount of £10,000, if he chose to suffer the arrest; and that too though the stoppage of the American trade was a greater loss to him than to any one else in the colony. Later on, an order came out for Nelson to be defended at the cost of the Crown, and so, for the time, Nelson's share in the business would seem to have ended; though for several years afterwards, new actions were entered and new writs issued, which, though always defended by the Crown, were meant to annoy and did annoy. But what perhaps annoyed most of all was the Treasury sending out their thanks to Sir Richard Hughes for his activity in protecting British commerce, while of Nelson's conduct no special notice was taken.

This question, which was as much legal or political as

naval, was still undecided when Nelson was again in difficulties with the Admiral about another of more technical
interest.   It was the custom of the Admiralty to appoint
to every dockyard at home or abroad a captain of the
Navy as commissioner or, as he would be now called,
superintendent, and this captain was generally, if not
always, on half-pay.   At this time the commissioner at
Antigua was Captain Moutray, a worthy old officer
without much service and that of no great distinction ;
though he had come prominently before the public
some five years before by having been, as captain of the
Ramillies, in charge of a very large, rich, and important
convoy which fell into the midst of the combined French
and Spanish fleet off Cape St. Vincent.   Moutray had
been tried for carelessness and dismissed his ship ; but
there was a strong feeling that the fault was really with
the Government for allowing such a valuable convoy to
go into the neighbourhood of the combined fleet without more efficient protection ; and after the change of
Ministry in 1782 Moutray had been appointed to this
commissionership as a sort of compensation.

Being on half-pay, he had, of course, no executive
authority ; but as, with ships continually coming and
going, the frequent change of senior officer appeared
to Hughes likely to cause inconvenience, he directed
Moutray to hoist a broad pennant as commodore, and
to take on himself the duties of senior officer in the port.
Now it was then, as it still is, an established rule in the
Navy that no authority but that of the Admiralty can
transfer an officer from half-pay to full-pay ; and as it
was perfectly well known that Moutray was on half-pay,
Nelson, coming to Antigua, ordered the broad pennant

to be struck, and sent Moutray notice that he could not take any orders from him until the Admiralty were pleased to put him on full-pay.

Moutray seems to have acquiesced readily enough, knowing, no doubt, that the order was an illegal one, and that his exercise of executive authority was irregular. But Hughes was furious at this second instance of insubordination, and reported the case to the Admiralty. So also did Nelson, with the result that he received a reprimand for his high-handed action. He ought, he was told, "to have submitted his doubts to the Commander-in-Chief, instead of taking upon himself to control Mr. Moutray's exercise of the functions of his appointment." A copy of the minute was sent to Hughes for his satisfaction; but as Moutray had been already ordered home, nothing more was done. At the present time the superintendent of a dockyard, whether at home or abroad, is always an executive officer on full-pay.

In both cases Nelson was right in his contention. Moutray had not, and under the circumstances could not have, any executive power; and the permission given to the American traders was in opposition to the Act of Parliament. On the other hand, it is easy to let our admiration for Nelson's later achievements blind us to the irregularity of his conduct from a service point of view. The first duty of an officer is to obey orders, to submit his doubts to the Commander-in-Chief, and in a becoming manner to remonstrate against any order he conceives to be improper; but for an officer to settle a moot-point himself, and to act in contravention of an order given under presumably adequate knowledge of the circumstances, is subversive of the very first principles of discipline. And these were not, it will be noticed, questions arising out of any sudden and unforeseen emergency, in providing for which Nelson was forced to depart from his instructions. Such emergencies do arise in the course of service, and the decision of the officer may be a fair test of his personal worth; but neither at St. Kitts nor at Antigua was there anything calling for instant decision, or any question which might not have waited, pending a reference to the Commander-in-Chief or to the Admiralty. And this was the meaning of the Admiralty minute on Nelson's conduct at Antigua, a most gentle admonition for what might have been punished as a grave offence. In themselves the matters were not of much consequence; but as marking Nelson's character at an early period, and illustrating his action in other and more important cases later on, they have a very special significance to any one wishing to examine the story of his career.

Not the least curious point about the dispute at Antigua is, that while refusing to accept Moutray's authority, and sternly and resolutely ordering Moutray's broad pennant to be struck, he was really on very friendly terms with Moutray himself, and was devotedly attached to Moutray's wife, who would seem, though we have no exact information, to have been many years younger than her husband. "Were it not for Mrs. Moutray, who is very, very good to me," Nelson wrote from Antigua, shortly after his arrival on the station, "I should almost hang myself at this infernal hole"; and again, in the middle of the dispute about Moutray's distinguishing pennant, he wrote to his brother: "My dear, sweet friend is going home. I am really an April day ; happy on her account, but truly grieved were I only to consider myself. Her equal I never saw in any country, or in any situation." It is in the same letter that, after giving an account of the young ladies on the station and their various little projects, he adds : " A niece of Governor Parry's has come out. She goes to Nevis in the *Boreas;* they trust any young lady with me, being an old-fashioned fellow."

A few weeks later, towards the middle of March, 1783, he sailed for St. Kitts, in the immediate neighbourhood of which he remained several months, and, as a relief from the troubles of the lawsuits with which he was pestered, fell in love with the niece of Mr. Herbert, the President of Nevis. Herbert's niece, Frances, the daughter of his sister and of William Woolward, a judge of the island, who had died in February, 1779, was at this time just twenty-four, having been born in the early part of 1761. In June, 1779, she had married Doctor Josiah Nisbet, who shortly afterwards became deranged, and died within eighteen months, leaving her with an infant son dependent on her uncle. During Nelson's former visit to St. Kitts he had not had an opportunity of making her acquaintance ; but now, very shortly after his return, he was brought to her notice by a letter from a young friend who wrote to her, probably from St. Kitts, in the middle or latter end of March : " We have at last seen the captain of the *Boreas*, of whom so much has been said. He came up just before dinner, much heated, and was very silent, yet seemed, according to the old adage, to think the more. He declined drinking any wine ; but after dinner, when the President, as usual, gave the following toasts, 'The King,'

'The Queen and Royal Family,' and 'Lord Hood,' this strange man regularly filled his glass, and observed that those were always bumper toasts with him ; which having drank, he uniformly passed the bottle, and relapsed into his former taciturnity. It was impossible, during this visit, for any of us to make out his real character ; there was such a reserve and sternness in his behaviour, with occasional sallies, though very transient, of a superior mind. Being placed by him, I endeavoured to rouse his attention by showing him all the civilities in my power ; but I drew out little more than 'Yes,' and 'No.' If you, Fanny, had been there, we think you would have made something of him ; for you have been in the habit of attending to these odd sort of people."

On May 12th, Nelson, writing to his brother, says incidentally that he has been visiting a young widow at Nevis ; and on June 29th, after writing, "The Admiral, Lady, and Miss sailed from here yesterday. Joy go with them ; I had rather have their room than their company "—adds a postscript : "*Entre nous.* Do not be surprised to hear I am a Benedict, for if at all, it will be before a month. Do not tell." Whether he was already an accepted lover it is impossible to say ; probably not, but at any rate he was so within a few weeks ; and a letter, written from Antigua on September 11th, begins "My dear Fanny," ends "Your affectionate," and discusses the prospect of their marriage in a calm, business-like manner. The whole tone of the letter, the first, apparently, he wrote to her, is rather esteem than passion ; it appears to be written by an affectionate friend rather than by an ardent lover. So much interest attaches to this point, the marriage has

been so often described as a genuine love-match, that it
may be well to reproduce this part of it. "I have
received a letter from Mr. Herbert, in answer to that
which I left at Nevis for him. My greatest wish is to
be united to you; and the foundation of all conjugal
happiness, real love, and esteem is, I trust, what you
believe I possess in the strongest degree towards you.
I think Mr. Herbert loves you too well not to let you
marry the man of your choice, although he may not be
so rich as some others, provided his character and situation in life render such a union eligible. I declare
solemnly that, did I not conceive I had the full possession of your heart, no consideration should make me
accept your hand. We know that riches do not always
ensure happiness : and the world is convinced that I am
superior to pecuniary considerations in my public and
private life; as in both instances I might have been
rich. But I will have done, leaving all my present
feelings to operate in your breast : only of this truth be
convinced, that I am your affectionate HORATIO NELSON.
P.S.—Do I ask too much when I venture to hope for a
line? or otherwise I may suppose my letters may be
looked on as troublesome." It was the natural sequel to
this letter that he should presently write one to his uncle,
whose promised assistance nearly two years before had
enabled him to propose to Miss Andrews. Mr. Suckling
was equally liberal on the present occasion, and agreed to
make him a sufficient allowance. What Nelson asked
for was £100 a year for a few years, and this was probably what was given. Nelson thought that Herbert
would give his niece two or three hundred a year during
his life, and he had promised to leave her £20,000 at his

death, or the bulk of his property, which was very great, if his own daughter should die before him.

The financial part of the negotiation being thus happily settled, the engagement was recognised; but the letters which Nelson wrote in his occasional absences from Nevis are, as a rule, remarkably sane, or even cool, for a newly-engaged lover. Some few, indeed, are more enthusiastic: some are as frantic as they ought to be ; but for the most part they might have been written to Collingwood or any other intimate friend. About the same date, too, he wrote to Mr. Suckling: "I have not an idea of being married till near the time of our sailing for England, which I did not think was to be till 1787 ; but report says—which I don't believe—we are to go home this summer."

The report was not true, and the *Boreas* remained sometimes at Nevis, sometimes at Antigua, occasionally at Barbadoes. From the biographical point of view these alternations were fortunate, as they gave rise to several interesting letters to Mrs. Nisbet. His life was meanwhile occupied with the ordinary routine, or with the lawsuits which continued to cause him much annoyance and to fill both his public and private letters. Climate and worry combined to wear out his health. "I am worn to a skeleton," he wrote to Mr. Suckling on July 5th, "but I trust that the doctors and asses' milk will set me up again"; and then follows a declaration which curiously confirms the former statement of Prince William as to the way in which the memory of his uncle Maurice was ever before him. "You have been my best friend, and I trust will continue as long so as I shall prove myself, by my actions, worthy of supplying that place in the service of my country which my dear uncle [Maurice] left for me. I feel myself, to my country, his heir; and it shall, I am bold to say, never lack the want of his counsel; I feel he gave it me as a legacy, and had I been near him when he was removed, he would have said, 'My boy, I leave you to my country. Serve her well, and she'll never desert, but will ultimately reward you.'"

In August Sir Richard Hughes went home, and Nelson was left senior officer on the station, so that when Prince William came out in November as captain of the frigate *Pegasus*, he was under Nelson's orders and resumed his former friendship with him; and learning that his chief was going to be married, he insisted that he must be present at the ceremony and give the bride away. Of the Prince Nelson formed a most favourable opinion, and most of his letters about this time, to Mrs. Nisbet, to his brother, or to Locker, are full of his praises. " In his profession he is superior to near two-thirds on the list " ; " In attention to orders and respect to his superior officers I hardly know his equal " ; " I wish that all the Navy captains were as attentive to orders as he is." Such are some of the expressions regarding the future king; and though much allowance must be made for Nelson's devoted loyalty and enthusiastic attachment to the Crown, his whole correspondence speaks to his high estimate of the Prince as an officer and a seaman.

On March 12th, 1787, Nelson was married, the Prince, as had been settled, giving the bride away. A month later Nelson wrote to the Admiralty that the *Boreas* was rotten, and would be too bad for the voyage if she did not sail before the hurricane season. The *Boreas* was not an old ship : she had been launched only thirteen years ; but the duration of wooden ships, more especially of those built during the ministry of Lord Sandwich, was very capricious. The state of the ship, however, made it necessary to recall her, and she arrived at Spithead on July 4th, 1787, Mrs. Nelson coming to England a passenger in a merchant-ship.

At the time our relations with France were very uncertain ; it was thought that war must break out at very short notice, and that therefore it was inexpedient to pay off the frigate. The fleet at Portsmouth was kept ready for sea, and had it sailed, the *Boreas* would have been attached to it. Nelson thought that nothing would be done that summer, but that war was almost certain to begin in the next year. In the middle of August the *Boreas* was sent round to the Nore, but with orders to be ready for sea at a moment's warning. In the middle of September he wrote : " We are here lying seven miles from the land on the impress service, and am as much separated from my wife as if I were in the East Indies. A war seems at present inevitable. . . . I suppose *Boreas* will be paid off, and her men put into some other ship, but what may become of me depends on Lord Howe. I always was for actual service, and should not like to be an idle spectator." Again, on October 3rd: "I have asked Lord Howe for a ship of the line, but *Boreas* is victualled for three months and ready for sea, ordered to hold myself in momentary readiness the moment my orders come on board."

His letters to his brother and Locker while lying at the Nore are frequent, and show no discontent at the

duty he was called on to perform, no particular irritation with the Admiralty; and there is absolutely no
reason to give the slightest credence to the story that in
his extreme disgust he determined to throw up his
commission and quit the service. Like many other
stories that have passed current, it probably grew up
out of the exaggerated repetition of some hasty remark.

The *Boreas* was paid off in the beginning of December,
and after a month in town arranging his affairs, Nelson
with his wife went to Bath. "I fear," he wrote, "we
must at present give [up] all thoughts of living so near
London, for Mrs. Nelson's lungs are so much affected
by the smoke of London, that I cannot think of placing
her in that situation, however desirable. For the next
summer I shall be down in Norfolk; from thence I must
look forward." Then he made a trip to Plymouth at
the invitation of Prince William, who had just come home
in the *Pegasus;* and writing to Locker, he repeated, in
an emphatic manner, his high opinion of the Prince as
an officer and seaman. "But," he added, "the great
folks above now see he will not be a cypher, therefore
many of the rising people must submit to act subordinate to him, which is not so palatable."

Late in the summer of 1788 Nelson went into
Norfolk, and, after a little hesitation, made his home
with his father at Burnham Thorpe, where, with a few
breaks, he lived for the next four and a half years. He
was still worried by lawsuits arising out of his conduct
in the West Indies, whether in relation to the seizure of
American traders or to the detection of frauds in the
supply of Government stores; and it was the end of
1789 before these were finally settled so far as he was

concerned.   Whether the Admiralty was altogether
pleased with his conduct has been doubted.   He was, it
is true, officially thanked by the several public Boards ;
but it is quite possible that he was marked as a man
likely to give trouble in time of peace by excess of zeal.
He himself thought that there was some pique against
him at the Admiralty, that Lord Hood was barely
civil to him ; and it is certain that his applications for
employment met with no response beyond a formal
acknowledgment.   The threatened rupture with Spain
on account of the seizure of English ships in Nootka
Sound, and that with Russia on account of the occupation of Otchakoff, blew over; ships were commissioned
and paid off, and Nelson was left unheeded.

There can be no doubt that he was at this time much
straitened in his pecuniary circumstances.   A captain's
half-pay was but small, about £120 a year, and this,
with Mr. Suckling's £100, was all that he had.   Whether
Mr. Herbert made his niece any allowance is nowhere
stated ; but we are permitted to suppose that monetary
considerations had a great deal to do with his ardent
desire to be appointed to a ship.   Meanwhile he led, we
are told, a life of almost idyllic retirement ; gardening,
digging, wandering in the woods with his wife, or
robbing birds' nests.   And a great part of his time was
spent in reading, writing, studying charts, drawing plans.
That he did read a good deal, more, much more, than
has been supposed, is very probable ; that he studied
charts and drew occasional plans is not improbable ; but
it is very unlikely that he wrote much, except letters,
and those at this period of his life were few.   In many
ways, however, this time of enforced retirement was of

advantage to him, and, by giving him opportunity for reading and reflection, completed the education which had been going on in a practical way ever since he left school at an age when education could scarcely have begun.

But he never ceased to wish for active employment, hopeless as it seemed to him. During the Spanish armament he called on Lord Hood, then a Lord of the Admiralty, and asked for his interest with Lord Chatham (the First Lord), that he might be appointed to a ship. Hood declined, and told him that "the King was impressed with an unfavourable opinion of him." "I cannot look on Lord Hood as my friend," he wrote in December, 1792; "but I have the satisfaction of knowing that I never gave his Lordship just cause to be my enemy." It is quite possible that he misunderstood this. Hood had formerly given him what he wanted, and was therefore his friend; now he could not grant his request, and therefore was no longer his friend. Probably Hood's feelings towards him were unchanged; but as he was some thirty-four years Nelson's senior, the commonplaces of intimacy and friendship were scarcely to be expected, and Hood was not one to put himself out to appear more amiable than he was. That he thought Nelson an able man, one to be relied on when real work was to be done, was shown by his immediately appointing him to a ship when a rupture with France was imminent. War was not declared till February 11th, 1793; but for more than a month it had been looked on as inevitable. On January 2nd the *Childers* brig, looking into Brest, was fired on: the shot was taken to the Admiralty, where Nelson saw it; and on the 7th, Lord Chatham, with many apologies, offered him the command of a 64-gun ship, if he would take it till there should be a 74 available. "After clouds comes sunshine," he wrote to his wife. "The Admiralty so smile upon me, that really I am as much surprised as when they frowned." On January 30th he was appointed to the *Agamemnon*.

CHAPTER III

CORSICA

THE commissioning of the *Agamemnon* was a very important era in Nelson's life. It may almost be spoken of as the beginning of his war-service; for what he had seen on the Spanish Main while in command of the *Hinchinbroke*, or in the West Indies while in the *Albemarle*, was scarcely worth mentioning, except that it had served to steady his own nerves and teach him how far he could depend on himself. He was now, after several years of reflection and of pondering over the mistakes and experiences of the past, making a fresh start with new officers, on a new station, and in very different circumstances. He was nearly thirty-four, but as yet his name was scarcely known outside his own family and the circle of his intimate acquaintance. To the Navy at large he could only be "the fellow that had the row with old Hughes"; and, with the exception of Hood, he could be little more to the Admiralty.

It was from the first understood that the *Agamemnon* was to go out to the Mediterranean as part of the fleet under the command of Lord Hood; but it was the end of April before she was ready to leave the Thames for Spithead. She was then sent for a cruise in the

Chops of the Channel, apparently to let the newly-commissioned ship shake down, though Nelson, in his impatience, wrote that she was "sported with merely to hum the nation." By May 23rd the fleet of eleven sail of the line under Hood's command was collected off the Lizard, and a fortnight later it proceeded on its way to Gibraltar and the Mediterranean.

Meantime, and in the manner natural to him, Nelson had been forming his opinion of the *Agamemnon,* her officers and men. He joined her on February 7th, and on the 10th wrote : "My ship is without exception the finest 64 in the service, and has the character of sailing most remarkably well. . . . The officers are all good in their respective stations and known to me, except the surgeon." On the 21st : "I am very much disposed to like Mr. Fellowes (the purser) and have told him so . . but that he must be very careful that no just cause of complaint can be made against him, for I will not suffer any poor fellow to be lessened of his due."

It may be necessary to explain that then, as all through last century and the first half of this, the chief part of the purser's emoluments was derived from the profit on the stores and slops which he issued ; that it was thus directly to his interest to issue short measures, and that he was almost always suspected of doing so ; that he was commonly referred to as "nip-cheese," and was said to choose his steward for the size of his thumb, so that by holding the measure with his thumb inside it, a respectable percentage of rum could be saved. Of course he was supposed to see that cloth, when being issued, was stretched to the point of rending ; and though these devices were perhaps much exaggerated in popular fancy, it is more than probable that a fraudulent agreement was frequently made with the contractor, by which cloth and clothes of an inferior quality were accepted and issued at the full price. Against such practices Nelson waged unceasing war, and took the earliest opportunity of letting the purser of the *Agamemnon* understand that he would not put up with any nonsense.

That Nelson was one of the most popular captains who ever commanded a ship is well known. But he was popular with his men not by pandering to their weaknesses and irregularities, but by a careful and continuous attention to their comforts and their rights ; he won the love of his officers not by tolerating neglect of duty, but by starting with the belief that they were all as determined as himself to do their duty to the utmost of their power, and that it was impossible he could be mistaken. It was thus that by April 18th he wrote: "I not only like the ship but think I am well appointed in officers, and we are manned exceedingly well, therefore have no doubt but we shall acquit ourselves well should the French give us a meeting. . . . With a good ship and ship's company, we can come to no harm. We appear to sail very fast." And on the 29th: "We are all well : indeed, nobody can be ill with my ship's company, they are so fine a set." In reality, of course, they were at first much the same as those of the other ships commissioned at the same time and manned in the same way. What they were after they had been a couple of years under the influence of Nelson is a very different thing.

On the way to Gibraltar, in order to save time, the

Agamemnon, with five other ships, was sent into Cadiz to
water; and Nelson had an opportunity of forming an
estimate of the Spanish navy. "We dined on board the
Concepcion, of 112 guns, with the admiral," he wrote on
June 23rd, "and all restraints of going into their
arsenals and dockyards were removed. They have four
first-rates in commission at Cadiz, and very fine ships,
but shockingly manned. If those twenty-one sail of the
line which we are to join in the Mediterranean are not
better manned, they cannot be of much use."

A fortnight later the English fleet fell in with the
Spanish off Alicante, twenty-four sail of the line. As
the English, on first seeing them, formed line of battle,
the Spaniards attempted to do the same, but after
several hours' trial did not succeed. Then, having made
out Hood's private signals, they sent down a frigate to
explain that they were very sickly; and no wonder, for
they had been sixty days at sea. Nelson thought this
ridiculous, for he wrote: "From the circumstance of
having been longer than that time at sea do we attribute
our getting healthy. It has stamped with me the extent of their nautical abilities; long may they remain in
their present state."

Nelson arrived at a right conclusion from false reason-
ing. The English seamen of 1793 were scarcely better
than those of 1778 when the fleet coming to Spithead after
a cruise of a couple of months off Ushant sent upwards
of four thousand men to hospital; and this had been
the rule. Nelson would seem also to have forgotten his
own cruise in the *Albemarle* in 1782. Hawke, indeed,
in 1759 had succeeded in keeping a fleet at sea and in
health for months together, but it was by a system of

constant reliefs; and Rodney in 1782 had been equally
fortunate, but the fleet was not continuously at sea. It
was only with the beginning of the war of the French
Revolution that, following the lessons taught by Captain
Cook, and by the rediscovery of the specific value of
lemon-juice, it became possible to keep a fleet healthy
without frequent refreshment. Hood's fleet had indeed
refreshed at Cadiz or Gibraltar, but independent of that,
its health seems to have been extraordinary. The mere
fact that the Spanish fleet of twenty-four sail of the line
had nineteen hundred sick on board after sixty days
at sea, was not in itself a proof of want of seamanship,
though the inability to form line of battle in several
hours might be considered so; and Nelson, putting together that fact, what he had seen at Cadiz, and what he
had heard of Rodney's action off Cape St. Vincent, was
fully justified in forming the conclusion that the Langara
of 1793 was no better seaman than the Langara of 1780,
and that the men he commanded were far from efficient.
It does not, however, appear that this conclusion was
generally accepted in the English fleet; and for several
years the Spanish navy was held to be as strong in
reality as in outward show.

In the middle of July the fleet arrived off Toulon,
and instituted a close blockade of that port and Marseilles.
Nelson wrote that "not a boat could get in, and the
old saying 'that hunger will tame a lion' was never
more strongly exemplified." On August 23rd commissioners were sent on board the flagship *Victory*, to
treat for peace on the basis of declaring a Monarchical
form of government in France; and a Republican army
having taken possession of Marseilles, Toulon surrendered

to the English, putting the citadel, the forts, and the ships at Hood's disposal. Langara with the Spanish fleet joined Hood just at this time, and the two together went into the harbour, while Nelson, in the *Agamemnon*, was hurriedly despatched to Naples to ask for and to bring back ten thousand troops to garrison the forts and hold the city.

This last he was not able to do; for, though the Neapolitan Government received him with open arms and readily promised the troops, just as preparations were being made for a visit from the King, the *Agamemnon* was hurried to sea by the news of a French ship of war being in the offing. Whether the news was false or not does not appear; but at any rate Nelson saw nothing of her, and hearing of a French 40-gun frigate at Leghorn, he put in there, hoping she might attempt to sail. This she would not do while the *Agamemnon* was there; and after waiting a few days for her, Nelson rejoined the Admiral at Toulon. The troops were meantime sent from Naples, and with them two ships of the line, one of which, the *Tancredi*, was commanded by the Chevalier Francisco Caracciolo, at this time an officer of good repute in the Neapolitan navy. By the middle of October Toulon was held by a force of upwards of twelve thousand men under the white flag of the Bourbons. But notwithstanding the numbers, the garrison had no cohesion, consisting as it did of so many different nationalities, all speaking different languages, with different interests, and recognising no one commander.

It is certain that the English in general, and probably Hood himself, believed Langara to be in treacherous communication with the Convention; and though there

does not seem to be any clear evidence of this, the
mere suspicion was in itself a marked element of weakness. Hood would have sent the French ships away;
but the Toulonese not unnaturally objected to this.
They were in arms against the Convention, not against
France, and believed that the revolt of Toulon was but
the prelude to the uprising of all France. The Spaniards
were equally opposed to the ships being taken possession
of by the English, and Hood, obliged to keep terms with
his allies whom he mistrusted, was unable to provide
for the security of the ships or of the city, as he would
fain have done. Thus it was that when the Republicans
attacked in force, they had little difficulty in rendering
themselves masters of the inefficient defences.

Then followed a scene of confusion and terror such
as has rarely been paralleled. Hood, seeing that the
place was untenable, gave orders for its evacuation, and
warned the inhabitants to provide for their safety. This
was on December 17th. It had already been determined
to burn the arsenal and the ships, men-of-war and
merchant-ships. The signal was made for the fleets to
put to sea; many of the ships, with their topmasts
struck, were busy refitting; one, the *Courageux*, was
hove down. They were got ready in a marvellously
short time, and hauled out into the roadstead. During
the 18th the English got their sick, wounded, and
soldiers on board without confusion; but the Spaniards,
Piedmontese, and Neapolitans were less able, and the
disorder became very great. The terror and despair of
the Toulonese were extreme. They sought to get on
board the English and Spanish ships of war, which received crowds: the *Princess Royal* had four thousand of

them on board, the *Robust*, three thousand ; others got
on board merchant-ships, fishing-boats, anything that
could float.   In all about fifteen thousand were able to
leave the town.   Many were drowned ; many were killed
by the shot from the French batteries.   Then night came
on ; the city and harbour were lighted up by the blazing
dockyard and a number of ships of the line, set on fire
by a party under the orders of Captain Sir Sidney
Smith.   The Spaniards had undertaken to set fire to
the ships in the inner basin ; but in the confusion and
consequent panic they neglected to do so, with one
exception, the powder-magazine.   This, which ought
of course to have been scuttled and sunk where she
was, was stupidly,—it cannot have been treacherously
—set on fire, and the terrific explosion increased
the panic.   During the night the fleets got into the
outer road, and put to sea on the 19th as the Republican
troops entered the town, to wreak a terrible vengeance
on the miserable remnant of the inhabitants, — the
old, the weak, women and children, who had been
unable to get on board any vessel.   The number who
perished,—killed during the siege, drowned on the night
of the 18th, or butchered afterwards by the victors—is
estimated at about six thousand.

With all this, however, Nelson had nothing to do.
On joining Hood on October 5th, he had been sent to
cruise on the coast of Corsica, and a few days later
received orders to join Commodore Linzee, Hood's
brother-in-law, off the south end of Sardinia.   In going
to the rendezvous, on October 22nd, off Cagliari, he fell
in with a squadron of five French ships, which proved
to be a brig, a corvette, and three large frigates.   One

of these last he cut off and brought to action; but her
consorts coming up, she joined them, and the *Agamemnon*
was in no case to pursue them.　The main topmast
was shot to pieces, mainmast, mizenmast, and foreyard
badly wounded, and the rigging much cut.　There is a
prevalent opinion that in the old war a frigate could not
and never did engage a ship of the line.　Of course it
is a mistake: scores of instances could be adduced to
prove that it is; and this is a very marked one.　The
frigate engaged, the *Melpomène*, though much damaged
herself, succeeded during a running fight in doing a
great deal of damage to the *Agamemnon*; and it appears
certain that a bolder conduct on the part of the other
two large frigates must have placed the *Agamemnon*
in a very awkward predicament.　The result of the
encounter, slight as it was, leaves no room to doubt
Nelson's opinion that they had a very great superiority
of force, and ought to have made a concerted attack on
him.　The French officers did not recognise this, and
were probably very well satisfied with getting away from
a 64-gun ship.

On joining Linzee, the little squadron of three 74-gun
ships, the *Agamemnon*, and two frigates went to Tunis,
where the business was to negotiate with the Bey, and
if possible bring away the French 80-gun ship *Duquesne*
together with some merchantmen.　Nelson, who believed
that the English never succeeded in a negotiation against
the French, was not surprised at their failure on this
occasion, and thought that they ought to have helped
themselves to the ships, and given the Bey £50,000 to
put up with the insult to his dignity; as it was, he
wrote, "We got nothing but being laughed at, and I

don't like it." He thought that Linzee had not shown as much decision in the matter as he might have done, and was well pleased when Hood, in "a very handsome letter," gave him an independent command of a frigate squadron on the coast of Corsica and Italy, to protect the trade, blockade Genoa, and look after the French frigates at San Fiorenzo,—the same that he had fallen in with on October 22nd. This was in the end of November, and on December 26th he was at Leghorn, whence he sent to the Admiralty the intelligence that reached him as to the loss of Toulon. A month later Hood, leaving the greater part of the fleet to watch Toulon, joined him on the coast of Corsica, which he had now determined to reduce.

A close blockade had been kept up by Nelson's squadron, and when the transports, after being scattered by a gale, were got together and the troops landed, San Fiorenzo surrendered without resistance on February 17th, the French garrison retiring to Bastia, which Hood wished to attack at once. On the 19th Nelson wrote to him that he had been looking at Bastia, and thought that, besides the seamen and Corsicans, they ought to have a thousand troops for a successful attempt. The General in command of the soldiers at San Fiorenzo, however, refused to make the attempt with all the men he had, about eighteen hundred, or until a reinforcement of two thousand men could be brought up from Gibraltar. With the force at their disposal, he considered the siege "to be a most visionary and rash attempt, and such as no officer would be justified in undertaking." Hood tried to argue the point; but as he could not command, the General remained firm, and refused to move.

Nelson had meantime made several desultory attacks on the seaward batteries, and had convinced himself that the place was not likely to make any prolonged resistance : one thousand men, he wrote, would certainly take it ; with five hundred and the *Agamemnon* he would attempt it. Hood was anxious to make the trial, but was unwilling to risk his ships in doing soldiers' work ; and it was only after Nelson's repeated assurances that the attempt was feasible, assurances supported by the opinion of two young officers, Lieutenant Duncan of the Artillery and Mr. de Butts of the Engineers, that he gave way. As the General refused to let him have any troops, with the exception of a few artillerymen, the work had to be done entirely from the fleet, from which the marines and soldiers serving as marines, nearly twelve hundred strong, were landed on April 4th, under the command of Lieutenant-Colonel Villettes of the Sixty-Ninth Regiment, and a party of two hundred and fifty seamen commanded by Nelson, with whom were Captains Anthony Hunt, Serocold, and Bullen. Six 13-inch and two 10-inch mortars were also landed, and ten of the *Agamemnon's* long 24-pounders. It was with these that the seamen were chiefly concerned ; they made the roads, they dug the trenches, they built the batteries, they cut down trees, they laid platforms, they dragged the guns into position, and when there they worked them. For so small a number of men the labour was extremely hard ; but they went about it with a will. The progress of the siege, however, was slow, the force employed in it being too small to permit the business to be hurried.

But meantime, with the assistance of a considerable

body of Corsicans, the investment on the land side was secure, and the blockade by sea was rigidly enforced. The garrison made several ineffectual attempts to obtain relief by boats; their provisions and ammunition were running short; they had many men killed and wounded, and many sick; and on May 19th they sent off a flag of truce with proposals to surrender. On the 24th the garrison, to the number of four thousand five hundred men, marched out and laid down their arms. Nelson wrote of "four thousand five hundred men laying down their arms to less than one thousand British soldiers who were serving as marines," and in the excitement of the moment it probably seemed so to him and those immediately concerned; but in his calmer moments no one knew better than he did that the success was mainly due to the action of the fleet, and that without it the small force on shore would have been altogether unequal to the task.

That much of the credit of the success belonged to Nelson must be admitted. Without his confidence Hood would scarcely have made the attempt; and his command of the seamen gave him a large share of the responsibility of what was done on shore. Hood, however, seems to have felt some difficulty in awarding the praise. It was clearly impossible for him in an official letter to speak his mind of the General's refusal to co-operate, or of his having himself yielded to the urgency of a subordinate; and of the work on shore he formed an estimate somewhat different from that of Nelson, who, in his familiar letters, described himself as having done the whole. He certainly did not command Villettes and the soldiers, who were to the seamen landed in the

ratio of four to one; and his own letters during the
siege show that there was some doubt whether he
commanded the batteries. On April 25th he wrote to
Hood, specifically stating that this doubt did exist, and
asking him for "an order to command the seamen without any distinction as to any particular services." It
does not, however, appear that he got such an order; and
the wording of Hood's despatch, "Captain Nelson, who
had the command and direction of the seamen in landing
the guns, mortars, and stores, and Captain Hunt, who
commanded at the batteries . . .," as well as of the
official note accompanying it, "Captain Hunt, who was
on shore in the command of the batteries," clearly implies that he did not. According to Southey, "Nelson's
signal merits were not so mentioned in the despatches
as to make them sufficiently known to the nation. . . .
This could only have arisen from the haste with which
the despatches were written." But the despatch was
dated May 24th, five days after the negotiations began,
and shows no signs of undue haste, either in these
sentences or in any other. That Nelson's services had
exceeded the strict limits of his command, that Hood
knew this and regulated his conduct thereby, is quite
another thing, which he did not think it fitting to
speak of in his public letters.

What gave Nelson almost as much gratification as the
fall of Bastia was the capture there of *La Flèche*, the
smallest of the frigate-squadron of the preceding October.
Two of the larger frigates had been sunk at San
Fiorenzo; but one, the *Minerve*, had been weighed, and
under the name of *San Fiorenzo* continued in the English
service during the war. The third frigate, the *Melpomène*,

with which the *Agamemnon* had been engaged, and the corvette, the *Mignonne*, were at Calvi, which Hood was now bent on reducing. But as he was getting ready for this new undertaking, he received intelligence that the French fleet, of nine sail of the line, had put to sea on June 5th, and that Vice-Admiral Hotham, who with seven sail was watching off Toulon, had fallen back to San Fiorenzo, considering the disparity of numbers too great. The disparity did not in fact exist, for the French fleet numbered only seven; but Hotham had not troubled to ascertain this, and Hood of course accepted the report. With six ships he sailed at once, joined Hotham on the 9th, and on the 10th sighted the enemy near St. Tropez. He could not prevent them going into the Golfe Jouan (which our older writers persistently miscall Gourjean Bay); but with a vastly superior force he resolved to go in and destroy them there, anchoring two ships against each one of the enemy.

Secure in his numbers, he had previously sent the *Agamemnon* back to carry on the arrangements for the siege of Calvi, meaning to follow so soon as the work immediately before him was finished. Unfortnnately the wind for several days rendered it impossible for him to go into Golfe Jouan; and when at last it permitted him, the enemy had made such use of the delay, by mounting guns on the islands which protected the anchorage, that he considered it unadvisable to make the attempt.

There were by this time nearly two thousand soldiers at Bastia, under the command of General Stuart, a man of a more enterprising character than his predecessors. Of these soldiers, fifteen hundred were now

embarked, escorted to the west side of the island, and
landed near Calvi on the 19th. About two hundred seamen from the *Agamemnon* and the transports were
also landed, and, as at Bastia, undertook the heavy
work of getting the guns into position. When Hood
with a part of the fleet arrived a few days later, more
seamen were landed, and with them Captains Hallowell
and Walter Serocold, the latter of whom had served
with Hunt in the batteries at Bastia, and was here
killed by a grapeshot on July 7th. After three weeks
of severe toil, the batteries opened fire upon the
town. For several days this was continued with little
intermission, Nelson and Hallowell, with whom he was
now for the first time intimately associated, taking
alternate twenty-four hours of duty at the advanced
battery. Many guns were broken or dismounted by
the enemy's fire; others were brought up in their place;
casualties were not infrequent. At 7 o'clock on the
morning of July 12th, a shot, striking the parapet of
the battery, dashed some sand and gravel against
Nelson's face, bruising his head and cutting the right
eye. The wound did not confine him, and the surgeons
gave him hopes that it would have no serious consequences. These hopes, however, were not realised, and
the sight of the damaged eye gradually faded away till
it was entirely lost. But meantime the siege continued,
and on August 1st the garrison agreed to surrender, if
not effectively relieved within ten days.

The negotiation was entirely in the hands of the
General. Nelson by no means approved of it; he would
have run under the bastion and blown it into the air in
less time. "I own," he wrote, "I had rather take a

place by our own fire and efforts than by the enemy being starved and sickly." On the 10th the garrison marched out with the honours of war, laid down their arms, and were embarked for a passage to France. The merchant-ships, the gunboats, and the frigates *Melpomène* and *Mignonne* also fell into the hands of the English. The two frigates were both added to the British Navy. The *Mignonne* proved unserviceable and was destroyed ; but the *Melpomène* continued effective during the war, and has transmitted her name through later ships to the present time.

Hood had already felt anxious about the French fleet at Toulon. He knew that several of the ships sunk or burned on December 18th had sustained little injury, and were being rapidly got ready for service in addition to the seven already blockaded in Golfe Jouan. Now that Calvi had fallen and the conquest of Corsica was complete, he rejoined the fleet. The *Agamemnon* was sent to Leghorn to refit, as well as to refresh her men, on whom the work of the siege had fallen heavily, and whose health now suffered. By the middle of September she again joined the Admiral off Toulon, and was immediately sent to Genoa, to protect and insist on the neutrality of the Republic. But her men continued very sickly ; in the middle of October she had still seventy-seven on the sick list, " almost all objects for the hospital."

It was by this time settled that Hood was to return to England, leaving the command temporarily to Vice-Admiral Hotham. The cause of this has never been shown, and it is uncertain whether it was for Hood's own convenience, or to enable him to confer with the

Government more freely than was then possible by letter. It was, however, clearly understood that he was to resume the command after a short absence.   That he did not do so was in consequence of a difference between him and the Admiralty as to the necessity of reinforcing the fleet, on which, and the neglect of the Admiralty, he expressed himself with what was considered undue vigour. When he resigned the command no other admiral was available; and it was thought that it might very well remain in the hands of Hotham, a man who had distinguished himself on several occasions during the American War, and was recognised as a brave man and a good officer.   In chief command, however, he was nervous, timid and undecided; "He is careful of us," wrote Nelson, "and will not suffer a line-of-battle ship to get out of his sight."

CHAPTER IV

By the end of January the French, having succeeded in bringing back their squadron from Golfe Jouan, had fifteen ships in the outer road of Toulon. To oppose these the English Admiral had thirteen under his command. In February a fourteenth joined him, as also the Neapolitan *Tancredi*, thus bringing the numerical number of the two fleets to a very close equality. "I wish Lord Hood would make haste out," wrote Nelson on March 2nd. On March 8th Hotham, then lying at Leghorn, received intelligence of the French being at sea. At daybreak the next morning he weighed with the fleet, thirteen sail of the line and the *Tancredi*. The *Berwick*, which had been at San Fiorenzo, in attempting to join the fleet at Leghorn had fallen in among the enemy on the 7th and been captured. During the 9th, 10th, and 11th the French fleet was repeatedly seen to the westward and reported by our frigates; but Hotham, whether with the intention of cutting them off from Toulon or not, stood to the northward and did not sight the enemy till the morning of the 12th. The fleet was then very much scattered, and in the light, fitful breeze was not able to get together. Admiral

Goodall formed the ships near him in a line of battle :
Hotham did the same ; but apparently nothing but the
incapacity of the enemy saved the English from a grave
disaster. " Our ships endeavouring to form a junction,"
was Nelson's description of the situation, "the enemy
pointing to separate us. They did not appear to me to
act like officers who knew anything of their profession."
Though they were bringing up a fresh southerly breeze,
they could neither form line of battle nor collect their
own fleet.

Late in the afternoon a fresh wind from the eastward
sprang up, and Hotham succeeded in forming his line of
battle towards the south, standing for the enemy's fleet.
The enemy were still in straggling disorder, and Nelson
thought that if the breeze held, our fleet would pass
through them, cutting off the van from the centre. But
the wind, which in these seas is very capricious, suddenly
flew round to the westward, and together with the darkness prevented immediate action. The next morning,
March 13th, the enemy's fleet was still in sight, a fresh
wind was blowing, and the signal was made for a general
chase. The French 84-gun ship *Ça Ira* carried away her
topmasts and fell astern. The *Inconstant* frigate, commanded by Captain Fremantle, attempted to cut her off,
but was unable to stand against the *Ça Ira's* heavy guns.
Two French ships then joined the *Ça Ira*, and a frigate
took her in tow. The *Agamemnon* was at this time well
up with them, and Nelson saw that, had he been
supported, it would have been possible to take the whole
four ; but no ship was near, and all he could do was to
attempt the destruction of the *Ça Ira* by keeping under
her stern, avoiding her very superior broadsides, and

yawing from time to time to pour in a raking and destructive fire. This went on for a couple of hours, at the end of which time the *Ça Ira* was a perfect wreck; but the enemy then came down in force to her rescue, Hotham made the signal for the van ships to join him, and for that day the *Ça Ira* was saved.

But the next morning the wind, continuing fresh, had shifted to the north-west, and given the weather-gage to the English, who were thus able to bring on a desultory action, and to cut off the *Ça Ira* in tow of the 74-gun ship *Censeur*. These two were speedily overpowered, and were taken possession of by a party from the *Agamemnon*. They had suffered most severely. The *Ça Ira* was completely dismasted, and was supposed to have three hundred and fifty killed and wounded; the *Censeur*, which had lost her mainmast, had lost about two hundred and fifty. The loss of men in the whole English fleet was less than that on board the *Ça Ira* alone; and though some of the English ships had their rigging cut and their masts wounded or shot away, the damage was relatively unimportant. The *Agamemnon* had been the most closely engaged, and of her Nelson wrote, "Our sails were ribbons, and all our ropes were ends"; but she had only six men wounded on the 14th, and seven on the 13th.

As to the action itself, it was Nelson's first experience. He had seen that the enemy with superior numbers would not push the fighting; he had judged that their officers were ignorant of their profession; he saw that they were unable to take advantage of the opportunity which had been given them. On the other hand, he had seen the danger to which the English were exposed

F

by having allowed themselves to drift asunder, and the loss which the country had sustained from their not being in a position to compel the enemy to abide their attack. At the time, he wrote to his uncle that, " Had the breeze continued so as to have allowed us to close with the enemy, we should have destroyed the whole fleet"; but to his wife, with greater freedom : " Had I commanded our fleet on the 14th, either the whole French fleet would have graced my triumph, or I should have been in a confounded scrape. I went on board Admiral Hotham as soon as our firing grew slack in the van and the *Ça Ira* and *Censeur* struck, to propose to him leaving our two crippled ships, the two prizes, and four frigates to themselves, and to pursue the enemy ; but he, much cooler than myself, said, ' We must be contented, we have done very well.' Now had we taken ten sail, and had allowed the eleventh to escape, when it had been possible to have got at her, I could never have called it well done. Goodall backed me ; I got him to write to the Admiral, but it would not do. We should have had such a day as, I believe, the annals of England never produced."

If this was his opinion at the time, we may be quite sure that further reflection but confirmed his judgment, and that during the months which followed he often asked himself how Locker's old chief would have conducted the business ; what Hood would have done ; or what he himself would have done, had he been indeed in command. The questions, too, had the added weight of his continually-growing conviction of Hotham's weakness. For a month after the battle the fleet lay at San Fiorenzo, leisurely refitting, while six French ships of the line, sent round from Brest under the command of

M. Renaudin, the captain of the *Vengeur* on the First of June, passed up and arrived at Toulon on April 4th. Nelson wrote of it to his father : " What the Admiralty are after to allow such a reinforcement to get out here, surprises us all " ; but in every letter at this time his cry was : " We are anxious to hear of Lord Hood's sailing from England " ; " We hope soon to see Lord Hood " ; " We have lost much by Lord Hood's going to England." And to his old captain, Locker, on May 4th he wrote : " Admiral Hotham is very well, but I believe heartily tired of his temporary command ; nor do I think he is intended by nature for a commander-in-chief, which requires a man of more active turn of mind." That the six ships were allowed to leave Brest may have been the fault of the Admiralty, or of the strain on the resources at their disposal ; but that they passed into Toulon unopposed was very clearly Hotham's fault ; and of that Nelson had no doubt, though he did not say it in so many words.

The Admiralty, having allowed six French ships to come into the Mediterranean, sent six English ships under Rear-Admiral Man to reinforce Hotham, whose fleet then consisted of twenty English ships and two Neapolitan. But on June 22nd Nelson wrote from off Minorca : " We have this day accounts of the French fleet's being at sea with twenty-two sail of the line and innumerable frigates, etc. We are waiting for our valuable convoy from Gibraltar, expected every moment ; are totally ignorant which way the enemy's fleet are gone ; hope sincerely they will not fall in with our convoy, but our Admiral takes things easy. Lord Hood's absence is a great national loss."

Meanwhile he was speculating on the probability of his getting his flag, of which he was much afraid, as likely to send him home and put him on half-pay : he hoped that instead of his flag he might get a colonelcy of marines, the pay of which would make a substantial addition to his income, and not interfere with his employment afloat. "It would suit me much better at present," he wrote. But his heart was sad, for each day his opinion grew stronger that under such a commander as Hotham no success was to be hoped for. On July 1st he wrote : "The French fleet of seventeen sail of the line are out, but only to exercise their men,—at least our good Admiral says so "; and referring to the capture of the French frigate *Minerve*, and the defeat of the *Artemise* by two very much smaller ships, the *Dido* and *Lowestoft*, "Thank God," he seemed to cry, "the superiority of the British Navy remains. I feel quite delighted at the event. Had our present fleet but one good chance at the enemy, on my conscience, without exaggeration, I believe that if the Admiral would let us pursue, we should take them all."

Three days later Nelson in the *Agamemnon*, with four or five frigates and small craft, was directed to go to Genoa, and to co-operate with the Austrian General in the Riviera. Off Cape delle Melle he fell in with the French fleet of seventeen sail, which chased him back to San Fiorenzo, where Hotham was lying, "having reason," he wrote, "to suppose that the enemy were certainly in Toulon," but having taken no pains to find out. When it was too late he wished to put to sea, but the wind prevented him, and it was not till the next day that he succeeded in getting out with twenty-three

ships of the line. The French, who had believed the
English to be still off Minorca, were disagreeably surprised to find them in their immediate neighbourhood,
and took advantage of the delay to make for their own
coast. They were thus not sighted till the 13th, being then
some six leagues south of the Hyères Islands. Hotham
made the signal for a general chase, but some six or
seven ships only got within range and engaged, till the
Admiral "judged it proper to call them off by signal,"
being apprehensive that they were too near the shore.
The wind was at the time blowing directly into the
Gulf of Frejus, where the enemy anchored after dark.
We may be perfectly sure that if Nelson had been in
command the English would have anchored with them.
That the opportunity of a complete victory, an annihilation of the French fleet, was offered them, he never
doubted : "To say how much we wanted Lord Hood at
that time is to say, Will you have all the French fleet or
no action? for the scrambling distant fire was a farce.
Hotham has no head for enterprise, perfectly satisfied
that each month passes without any losses on our side."

So soon as the action was over and there was no
longer any possibility of his being interfered with by
the French fleet, Nelson was again sent on his former
mission to Genoa and the Riviera, a detached service on
which he continued with little intermission for more
than a year. And peculiarly active service it was,
though of a nature which it would be tedious to relate in
detail. It was difficult moreover in its political relations ;
for Genoa, nominally neutral, was overawed by the
French, who used the country for their own purposes
and forbade any favour to their enemies. The Genoese

had no doubt that severe punishment would follow
their disobedience ; they believed that the English would
be a more generous enemy, and made their choice
accordingly.   What Nelson had before him was to
thwart the designs of the French ; to stop their coasting
trade, on which the south of France was largely dependent for its supplies, corn, vegetables, and such like ;
to prevent their troops or provisions of war being
transported by sea, or so far as possible by land ; and to
do all this without giving the Genoese just cause to complain of a violation of their neutrality.   In this he was
guided by the advice of Mr. Trevor and Mr. Drake, the
Ministers at Turin and Genoa, but from Hotham he seems
to have received neither counsel nor assistance.   "However," he wrote, "political courage in an officer abroad is
as highly necessary as military courage " ; and acting on
that maxim, constituted himself virtually independent
and Commander-in-Chief of the inshore squadron.
Within a month he wrote : "The French army is now
supplied with almost daily bread from Marseilles ; not
a single boat has passed with corn.   The Genoese are
angry, but that does not matter."

The rule which he laid down was that any part of the
Riviera occupied by the French army should be considered enemy's country and be treated as such ; that, in
fact, the pretence of neutrality should not shelter the
French army or its operations ; and acting on this, on
August 26th he seized a 10-gun corvette, with some
armed boats and eight store-ships, at Alassio.   On the
31st he wrote : "The Genoese are going, it is said, to
carry a convoy with provisions to their towns in the
Riviera of Genoa, in possession of the French army.

However cruel it may appear to deprive poor innocent
people of provisions, yet policy will not allow it [not] to
be done; for if the inhabitants have plenty, so will the
enemy, and therefore I have directed them to be brought
into Vado. . . . Our Admiral, *entre nous*, has no political
courage whatever, and is alarmed at the mention of any
strong measure; but, in other respects, he is as good a
man as can possibly be." Many of his most interesting
letters at this time are written to Sir Gilbert Elliot,
the English Viceroy of Corsica, afterwards Earl of
Minto and Governor-General of India, with whom he had
contracted a friendship which lasted through life. It
seems, in fact, that, in want of a Commander-in-Chief on
whom he could depend, he turned to Elliot for advice or
suggestions as to the diplomatic entanglements which
strewed his path. Not indeed that he allowed these to
trouble him too much; but it was no doubt comforting
to him to find the chief representative of the Foreign
Office in the neighbourhood taking his view of the
question. He would gladly have done more than he
did, but his force was insufficient, and Hotham would
not increase it. "I only want transports," he wrote to
Elliot on September 24th, "and if he gave me one 74,
I verily believe we should yet possess Nice." But
Hotham made no sign; and the Austrians naturally
complained that they had been brought to the coast at
the express desire of the English, to co-operate with the
fleet which they never saw, while the detached squadron was so miserably insufficient or ineffective that it
had not been able to prevent the French gunboats from
harassing their left wing in the Bay of Loano, where no
gunboats should have been allowed.

Nelson had no difficulty in showing that the loss they complained of was none of his doing ; that one 64-gun ship, whose presence at Genoa was clearly wanted and was emphatically demanded by the imperial Minister, could not be also at Pietra ; that the frigates which he had left for that service had been taken away without his knowledge ; and that though the gunboats annoyed their retreat, they had nothing to do with their defeat which began with the right wing twelve miles inland. He was anxious to justify himself to the Austrian General, and sent a letter for him to Mr. Drake ; which, however, Drake did not forward, submitting to Nelson whether it was proper to offer any justification of his conduct to a foreign general. Besides, he continued, "anxious as the Austrian Generals are to transfer the blame of the misfortunes of November 23rd from themselves to us, they have always done ample justice to your zealous and able conduct ; their complaints turn upon the insufficiency of the force under your command, and not upon the mode in which that force was employed."

This insufficiency of his force was exactly what Nelson had striven against ; nor had he forgotten it five years later, when he wrote to Lord Keith, then preparing for the siege of Genoa : " You will now bear me out in my assertion, when I say that the British fleet could have prevented the invasion of Italy ; and at that time we had nothing to do. If our friend Hotham had kept his fleet on that coast, I assert, and you will agree with me, no army from France could have been furnished with stores or provisions ; even men could not have marched." That the fleet was doing nothing, and might have been commanding the Riviera, is certain ; but the presence of a large French fleet at Toulon gave Hotham the excuse of having to keep watch on it, and so not being able to spare Nelson any reinforcements ; as to which Captain Mahan has aptly remarked : "Hotham could better have spared ships to Nelson if he had not thrown away his two opportunities of beating the Toulon fleet."

It is indeed difficult to realise the enormous difference which would have been made in the history of the war if the French fleet had been destroyed on July 13th, as Nelson at the time thought it might and should have been destroyed, and as we, reading the story of the battle by the light of what Nelson did three years later, now see was a perfectly feasible operation for any commander of strong resolution.   With that fleet destroyed, the Riviera would have been effectively guarded : men could not have marched ; stores could not have passed ; Italy could not have been invaded.   Neither Loano nor Montenotte would have been fought, and Bonaparte's patent of nobility would have had to be sought elsewhere ; the history of Italy for the next twenty years, and for all time, would have been cast in a different mould ; Spain would have remained true to the English alliance, and the French expedition to Egypt would have remained undreamed of.   That the rise and grandeur of Bonaparte's career are thus bound up with Hotham's irresolution on July 13th, has perhaps not been so generally noticed or understood as the interest of the fact deserves ; but in this sense that "miserable action," as Nelson called it, appears more worthy than Valmy of being styled a decisive battle.

Hotham had meantime written to be recalled, on the plea of ill-health, and Sir John Jervis was at once named as the fitting successor. As captain of the *Foudroyant* in the War of American Independence, Jervis had distinguished himself by the perfection of the discipline and order of his ship, the beauty and value of which had shone forth with redoubled splendour in the easy capture of the French *Pégase*. He had afterwards taken a leading part in the opposition to Pitt's fancy for resting the defence of the south coast on fortifications, maintaining that, though these fortifications might be advisable or even necessary if the fleet was absent from England, the assumption that it would be absent, leaving the enemy to operate freely in the Channel, was practically absurd. On the outbreak of the present war, he had been sent as Commander-in-Chief on the Leeward Islands station, where he had reduced Martinique, Saint Lucia, and Guadeloupe, and had shown a marvellous force of character and power of command. He was now, at the ripe age of sixty, sent out to command the Mediterranean fleet at a time when, by Hotham's mismanagement, the situation was every day becoming more critical. The Spanish Government, unable to resist the pressure of the French arms in the north of Spain, and not improbably influenced by money paid to Godoy, had made peace with France, and would, it was believed, shortly form a defensive and offensive alliance; while the French fleet by itself was numerically superior to the English, which the requirements of the Channel, the West Indies, and other stations rendered it impossible to reinforce.

On November 12th, 1795, Jervis in the *Lively* frigate

sailed from Spithead, and arrived at Gibraltar on the
23rd. He was there met by Rear-Admiral Man, who
had been sent with a detached squadron to cruise off
Cadiz, where seven French ships of the line and three
frigates were lying in friendly association with the
Spanish fleet. Jervis now confirmed Man's orders, and
went on to join the fleet in San Fiorenzo Bay on the
29th. He had not improbably already formed the
opinion that the fleet had seen too much of San Fiorenzo
Bay, and before the smoke of the salute to his flag had
blown away, made the signal to unmoor. It was the signal
of a new order of things; of a strictness of discipline
in all departments, of an activity on service and a restless energy, such as had never been equalled, and which
brought the fleet to a point of unparalleled efficiency.
And it was off an enemy's port that this reformation
was carried on. In January the fleet took up its station
off Toulon, the inshore squadron being seldom more
than three miles from the entrance to the harbour,
while the force under Jervis's personal command was,
as a rule, smaller than that inside the harbour, which
consisted of fifteen sail of the line. Jervis had indeed
under his command twenty-five ships of the line; but
seven of these were with Man off Cadiz, and others were
employed on different and constantly varying services
in different parts of the station. Troubridge, for instance, with the *Culloden* and some frigates, was sent to
the Archipelago in December to look after Ganteaume,
who had been allowed to escape from Toulon; and in
March Vice-Admiral Waldegrave with five sail was at
Tunis, bringing out the *Nemesis* frigate, which Ganteaume had captured and sent there.

By the occupation of the Riviera after the battle of
Loano, Nelson's immediate work was brought to an
abrupt conclusion, and he went to Leghorn to refit his
ship. On January 19th, 1796, he joined the Admiral,
whom he now saw for the first time, and was received, as
he wrote, "not only with the greatest attention but with
much apparent friendship." As the *Agamemnon*, after
being three years almost always under way, was getting
very crazy, Jervis offered him either the 90-gun ship *St.
George* or the *Zealous*, a 74. Nelson preferred to remain
in his old ship, being unwilling to leave the officers and
men who had shared with him this long and arduous
service. The very next day he was sent again into the
Gulf of Genoa to prevent the passage of the enemy's
troops by sea; and during the following months was
almost constantly on the move, ranging the coast from
Toulon to Leghorn. It was at this time his fixed idea
that the French, having an apparent superiority, would
try to force a passage by sea, and land their army towards Leghorn, when there would be nothing to stop
their progress to Rome and Naples. They had in Toulon
thirteen ships actually ready for sea, and four or five
more in great forwardness. Nelson thought that they
would endeavour to bring back the ships from Cadiz, and
probably also others from L'Orient or Brest. "We may
fight their fleet," he wrote, "but unless we can destroy
them, their transports will push on and effect their
landing. What will the French care for the loss of a
few men-of-war? It is nothing, if they can get into
Italy. This [is] the gold mine, and what, depend on it,
they will push for."

We know now, what neither Jervis nor Nelson knew

then, that the appearance of the French fleet was a
delusion, that the best ships had gone with Richery, and
that those which remained were in bad condition, badly
manned, and in no state to engage a fleet such as that
under Jervis's command.   The French officers were quite
conscious of their absolute inferiority, and it does not
appear that the idea which filled Nelson's mind was
entertained by them ; if they discussed it, it was at
once given up as impracticable, and the advance by land
determined on.   Montenotte was fought on April 12th,
and a few days later peace was concluded by the
Sardinians.   Everything seemed to show that Spain
was going to join France, and in that case, Nelson
thought, Naples would do the same.   "Should all the
powers in this country make peace," Nelson wrote to
Sir Gilbert Elliot on May 16th, "and the French possess
themselves of Leghorn and other places to cut off our
supplies, Corsica will be the only tie to keep our great
fleet in the Mediterranean ; how far the conduct of those
islanders, taken in a general scale, deserves that a fleet
and army should be kept for their security, is well
deserving of serious consideration."

In the end of March the Admiral ordered Nelson
to wear a distinguishing pennant, constituting him, as it
would be now called, a commodore of the second class ;
he actually hoisted it on April 4th.   It did not, however,
make any change in his duties : that was produced by
the march of events ; and on May 15th he wrote to
Jervis : "Do you really think we are of any use here ?
If not, we may serve our country much more by being
in other places.   The Levant and coast of Spain call
aloud for ships, and they are, I fancy, employed to no

purpose here; for unless the Austrians get possession of a
point of land, we cannot stop the coasting trade." On the
18th he wrote again: "Money, provisions, and clothes the
enemy have in abundance; and they command arsenals
to supply their wants in arms and ammunition." Still,
though he could not control the enemy, he could annoy.
"I have got," he wrote on June 2nd, "the charts of
Italy sent by the Directory to Bonaparte; also Maille-
bois' *Wars in Italy*, Vauban's *Attack and Defence of Places*,
and Prince Eugene's *History;* all sent for the General.
If Bonaparte is ignorant, the Directory, it would appear,
wish to instruct him; pray God he may remain ignorant." And so the peculiar service on which he had been
so long engaged came to an end.

The state of the *Agamemnon* rendered it necessary
that she should go to England before the winter; and
Nelson was almost daily expecting his promotion to flag
rank, which he feared might put him on half-pay. Jervis
virtually undertook that, if he was promoted, he should
hoist his flag in the Mediterranean fleet, and meantime
appointed him to the 74-gun ship *Captain*, her former
captain, who was in bad health and anxious to go home,
moving into the *Agamemnon*. Nelson joined the *Captain*
on June 11th, and after two or three days at Genoa
was sent to Leghorn, then threatened by the French.
Captain Fremantle, in the *Inconstant*, was already there,
and by great exertions had got all the English residents
and their property safe on board ship and out of the port
before the French entered. Nelson was now ordered to
blockade it; for the better performance of which service,
and at the request of Sir Gilbert Elliot, he took possession
of the island of Elba. A few days later he was able

to write : "The blockade of Leghorn is complete ; not a vessel can go in or come out without my permission." This, he thought, would soon make the Grand Duke repent his admission of the French; and in fact the total stoppage of the trade, the great number of men thrown out of employment, and the absolute want of food, raised such a feeling that the French would probably have been driven out, had not the defeat of the Austrians at Lonato and Castiglione altered the position.

The interest then turned on the policy of Spain. For months Nelson's letters repeat that war is spoken of as probable. "I have my doubts as to it," he wrote to the Admiral, "but if it is, with your management I have no fears as to any fatal consequences. The Spanish fleet is ill manned, and worse officered, I fancy." And to his father, on August 18th : "The only consequence it can be to us may be the necessary evacuation of Corsica, and that our fleet will draw down the Mediter-ranean. The Dons will suffer in every way for their folly if they are really so foolhardy as to go to war to please the French." Corsica, he thought, must go in any case, for the French had a strong party in the island ; many Corsicans were officers in the French army, and it was impossible to hinder French troops getting over by twenty or thirty at a time. As to the fleet, nobody, he thought, could have any fear under an admiral such as Jervis. The English had twenty-two ships of the line ; France and Spain joined would not have more than thirty-five. "I will venture my life," he said, "that Sir John Jervis defeats them." But on August 27th he wrote to Elliot: "I own I cannot even yet bring myself to believe that the Spaniards will go to war with us."

War was not, in fact, declared till October 5th, but for some weeks it was practically certain that it was going to be declared. It was known that Spain had concluded an offensive and defensive alliance with France, and that English ships had been stopped in Spanish ports. On September 25th Jervis received an order "to co-operate with the Viceroy in the evacuation of Corsica, and with the fleet to retreat down the Mediterranean." He lost no time in directing Nelson, whom on August 11th he had appointed a commodore of the first class, to take charge of the evacuation, which was carried out by October 19th. But although Nelson had anticipated the measure, as well as the possibility of leaving the Mediterranean, now, when the time came, the appearance of being driven out was very bitter to him. "I lament our present orders," he wrote, "in sackcloth and ashes, so dishonourable to the dignity of England, whose fleets are equal to meet the world in arms." Neither he nor the Admiral, however, considered Corsica tenable; and when, towards the beginning of November, Jervis received counter-orders to hold Corsica if not already evacuated, he replied that it was "a great blessing" that the evacuation had already taken place; for it would have been impossible to hold it for any length of time against the feeling of the Corsicans, and without a tenable post in the island.

The fleet was a different thing, and with that it was his intention to remain. With Elba as a base, and with his full numbers collected together, he felt himself quite equal to the task of making head against the combined fleet, even if they had combined ; or of defeating either singly, if he could meet it on its way to combine. He had accordingly sent orders to Man, then at Gibraltar, to join him at once with his whole force ; nor had he doubted that these orders would be obeyed, till, on November 11th, he learned that, on receiving them, Man had judged them impracticable and had taken his squadron to England. This serious defection left Jervis no alternative. With no interests to protect, no allies to defend, only fourteen ships of the line with which to meet thirty-eight, and no secure port to fall back on in case of reverse, his only available course was to retire on Gibraltar. And this, accordingly, he did.

CHAPTER V

ST. VALENTINE'S DAY

On December 1st, 1796, the fleet under Sir John Jervis anchored in Gibraltar Bay. A week later he received instructions to provide specially for the protection of Portugal, and to complete the evacuation of the Mediterranean by withdrawing the garrison from the island of Elba. This duty was entrusted to Nelson, who shifted his broad pennant to the *Minerve* frigate, and with the *Blanche* in company, sailed from Gibraltar on December 15th. Off Cartagena, on the evening of the 19th, they fell in with two Spanish frigates, which they engaged and captured. The one which struck to the *Minerve* was the *Santa Sabina*, commanded by Don Jacobo Stuart, a descendant of the Duke of Berwick. Scarcely was she taken possession of, when another frigate came towards them; it was then half-past three in the morning, and in the dark she was mistaken for the *Blanche*, till she hailed the *Sabina* in Spanish and, finding her in the possession of the English, fired a broadside into her. The *Minerve* had the *Sabina* in tow, but at once cast her off and engaged the stranger, which attempted to make off, followed by the *Minerve*. At daylight, however, the relation was changed. Two Spanish ships of the line

and another frigate came on the scene; and the four
now chased the *Minerve*, whose capture appeared imminent. She was saved by the presence of mind of
Lieutenants Culverhouse and Hardy on board the *Sabina*,
who reminded the Spaniards of their loss by hoisting
the English colours with the Spanish below them. This
was more than the Spaniards could stand, and the largest
of the line-of-battle ships turned aside to recapture the
frigate. But it was a couple of hours before she could
do this; and though the others continued the chase,
they were gradually left astern by the *Minerve*. The
Blanche had not had time to take possession of her prize,
and escaped unpursued.

On the 26th Nelson anchored at Porto Ferrajo, but
found that General de Burgh, in command of the troops,
did not think himself authorised to abandon the place
without positive orders, though he was clear that no
good was to be gained by staying, now that Naples had
made peace with France and the English fleet had
quitted the Mediterranean. Nelson accordingly collected
the ships which had remained behind, embarked the
naval stores, and, on receiving a final refusal from General
de Burgh, left with him a few small craft under the
command of Captain Fremantle in the *Inconstant*, and
sailed on January 29th, 1797, Sir Gilbert Elliot and
his staff taking a passage in the *Minerve* or other vessels
of the squadron. After looking into Toulon where the
French fleet still lay, and into Cartagena from which
the Spanish fleet was absent, Nelson was in feverish
haste to rejoin the Admiral, and on February 9th
anchored at Gibraltar.

Three Spanish ships were lying at Algeziras, and

from these he received the two lieutenants Culverhouse and Hardy, who had been taken in the *Sabina*, in exchange for Don Jacobo Stuart, previously sent into Cartagena with a flag of truce. The *Minerve* sailed on the forenoon of the 11th, and was immediately followed by two of the Spanish ships, which hoped to make an easy capture of the frigate. By an accident they had success within their reach. Running through the Straits with a fair wind, the *Minerve* lost a man overboard. The jolly-boat was lowered, with Lieutenant Hardy and her crew on board, but the man had sunk, and was never seen again. The jolly-boat was now found to be in great danger, for the ship still held her way, and the easterly current was setting the boat fast astern, while the leading Spanish ship was coming up under a full spread of canvas. With an anxious eye Nelson took in the situation. "By God," he cried, "I'll not lose Hardy; back the mizen topsail!" As the ship came to, the Spaniards, astounded at the manœuvre, could only interpret it as meaning that she saw the English fleet coming in from the westward; and not choosing to incur the risk of meeting with them, hauled their wind and stood back to the eastward, while the *Minerve*, having picked up the jolly-boat, resumed her course, passed through the Spanish fleet during the night of the 12th, and on the 13th joined the Admiral off Cape St. Vincent, giving him the news of the near approach of the Spaniards. The same afternoon Nelson shifted his broad pennant back to the *Captain;* and at daybreak the next morning the Spanish fleet was seen some fifteen or twenty miles to the southward. The weather was extremely hazy, and it was nearly eleven before the look-out vessel could signal that there were twenty-five ships of the line; two were presumably shrouded in the fog, for there were really twenty-seven.

Since coming to Gibraltar the English fleet had received several important reinforcements to make up for the deficiency caused by Man's absence; but a succession of untoward losses had prevented its numbers being increased. Two ships had been totally lost; one, with a great lump of rock driven through her bottom, had been sent to England; two others had been docked at Lisbon. It was thus that, on the morning of St. Valentine's Day, February 14th, 1797, when Jervis met the Spanish fleet on its way northwards, with the intention of joining the French at Brest, he had with him only fifteen sail of the line; and though nine of them had been subject for the past year to his iron discipline, the odds against him still appeared excessive. But he knew that the state of affairs at home rendered it necessary at all hazards to prevent the Spaniards from going to Brest. "A victory is very essential to England at this moment," he was heard to mutter as he paced the *Victory's* quarter-deck; then, as he drew near and saw the enemy's fleet, with the wind at west by south, straggling across the line of his advance, he formed his fleet in line of battle towards the south, and steered for a gap between two of the enemy's divisions, so as to cut off seven of their ships to leeward. The western division was running down to join them, and two three-decked ships succeeded in doing so. The rest, seeing that they were too late, wore all together and stood to the north, firing some distant shots at the English line as they passed on opposite tacks. But as the leading ship, the *Culloden*, commanded by Troubridge, Nelson's old companion in the *Seahorse*, came into the wake of the Spaniards, Jervis made the signal to tack in succession; and the *Culloden*, fully prepared for the order, came round at once and fell among the rear of the retreating Spaniards.

It has often been pointed out that the particular manœuvre which Jervis had ordered was a tactical blunder; for, according to the signal, each of his ships was bound to stand on till she reached the spot where the *Culloden* had tacked before she could follow. This gave the enemy time to get some considerable distance ahead, so that, to all appearance, the action would end in a desultory interchange of firing, without any decisive result. There are many who think that what Jervis should have signalled in the circumstances was to tack all together, that is, each ship where she actually was when the signal was made; and had this been done, there can be little doubt that the battle would have been much sharper and more decisive than it was. That it was so in any degree was due not to Jervis but to Nelson, whose ship, the *Captain*, was in the rear of the fleet, the last but two; and seeing that by the manœuvre ordered, not only could the *Captain* not get into action, but also that the Spaniards, as they passed clear of the sternmost ships, were bearing up to run down to leeward and join the other division, he took on himself, not for the first time, to disobey the order, wore out of the line, and stood on the other tack to meet the Spanish Admiral in the *Santisima Trinidad*, the largest ship then afloat, which, as well as the other ships with him, he compelled to haul to the wind again. The delay enabled the *Culloden* and the other leading ships to come up ; and Jervis, partly recognising his mistake, signalled the *Excellent*, the rearmost ship, also to tack. The action thus became more general. Two of the Spanish ships struck their colours and were taken possession of. The rest fled.

After engaging the *Santisima Trinidad* and several others, the *Captain* was then in close action with the *San Nicolas* of 84 guns. She had suffered much in her rigging, and was apparently hard pressed by her huge antagonist, when Collingwood in the *Excellent*, passing between the two, poured a tremendous broadside into the Spaniard at a distance of only a few feet. The *San Nicolas* luffed up, possibly to prevent the *Excellent* fouling her ; and in so doing fell on board the three-decker *San Josef*, which apparently bore up at the same moment to avoid the fire of the *Prince George ;* and the two, having already suffered severely, lay practically helpless. The *Captain* also was almost unmanageable, "her foremast gone, not a sail, shroud, or rope left, her wheel shot away " ; and Nelson, seeing her unable to follow the flying Spaniards, ordered the helm to be put a-starboard and called for the boarders. As the *Captain's* spritsail yard hooked in the mizen rigging of the *San Nicolas*, Berry, who had been first lieutenant of the *Agamemnon* and the *Captain*, and having been promoted shortly before, was now serving as a volunteer, sprang into her mizen chains and scrambled on board, closely followed by Lieutenant Pierson of the Sixty-Ninth Regiment and his soldiers. The upper quarter gallery window was dashed in, and Nelson himself with others jumped through. A few pistol-shots were fired, but the resistance was little more than nominal ; and while Berry on the poop hauled

down the Spanish flag, Nelson with Pierson and some
of his men went forward, where the officers, already
prisoners to some of the *Captain's* seamen, delivered
up their swords.

At this moment some muskets were fired from the
stern-walk of the *San Josef*, and Nelson, directing the
soldiers to fire into her stern, called for more men and
proceeded to board the three-decker. Berry assisted
him into her mizen chains, when a Spanish officer
looked over the side and said they surrendered. Nelson
was quickly on the quarter-deck, where the captain
presented his sword, saying that the admiral was below,
dying. But the other Spanish officers were called up
and delivered their swords, which, wrote Nelson, " as I
received, I gave to William Fearney, one of my barge-
men, who put them under his arm with the greatest
sang-froid." The *Victory* and the other ships, as they
passed the *Captain*, cheered her ; and when Nelson, after
shifting his broad pennant to the *Irresistible*, went on
board the *Victory*, the Admiral, according to Nelson's
own account, "received me on the quarter-deck, and
having embraced me, said he could not sufficiently thank
me, and used every kind expression, which could not fail
to make me happy."

After four years' service in the *Agamemnon* and the
Captain, Nelson's reputation as a man of courage and
ability was very well established ; but this day had
shown him in a still more favourable light, and had
presented him as a man no less quick to discern than
prompt to act. It was thus that Collingwood, who had
long been on terms of intimate friendship with him,
wrote the next day : " It added very much to the satis-

faction which I felt in thumping the Spaniards, that I
released you a little. The highest rewards are due to
you and *Culloden ;* you formed the plan of attack, we
were only accessories to the dons' ruin; for had they
got on the other tack, they would have been sooner
joined, and the business would have been less complete."
But more than this, the battle brought his name prominently before the country. The news of the victory
reached London on the afternoon of March 3rd, and the
same evening a vote of thanks to Jervis and all under
his command was carried by acclamation in the House
of Commons. An intolerable weight was taken off the
country ; and as people began to ask about particulars
they learned that a captain of a 74 had carried by
boarding first an 80 and then a 112-gun ship, and that
his coxswain had collected the swords of the Spanish
officers under his arm " as if he was making up a faggot."
It was this, the apparent disproportion of the combatants
to the magnitude of the results, that caught the popular
fancy, and Nelson was at once installed as the ideal of a
naval hero. Even now, misled by exaggerated descrip-
tions and imaginative pictures, it is very commonly
supposed that he captured the two Spaniards in a
desperate hand-to-hand conflict amid the clash of
cutlasses and dint of tomahawks : people do not stop now,
any more than they did then, to reflect that what Nelson
did was, with great resolution and vigour, but without
any serious fighting, to take forcible possession of two
beaten ships, which but for his prompt action would very
probably have got away, as the *Santisima Trinidad* and
other beaten ships actually did. Nelson himself, who
was by no means given to minimise his exploits, did not

claim to have done anything more, and though he wrote :
" There is a saying in the fleet too flattering for me to
omit telling,—' Nelson's patent bridge for boarding first-
rates,' alluding to my passing over an enemy's 80-gun
ship," he wrote also more modestly : " I pretend not
to say that these two ships might not have fell had I not
boarded them; but truly it was far from certain but
they might have forged into the Spanish fleet as the
other two ships did."

There is no question that the capture of the *San
Nicolas* and *San Josef* did illustrate Nelson's genius,
though not in the way that fancy has represented.
Undaunted courage of course he had, but so also had
scores of officers and men in the fleet; the quick perception that the ships were beaten, that the *Captain* was
useless in the chase, the determination not to lie idle
when anything could be done,—all this was Nelson's own.
But a higher and finer display of the same quickness of
perception, the same prompt resolution, with the utter
fearlessness of responsibility, was given in the wearing
out of the line without orders, and throwing himself, all
unsupported, in the way of the *Santisima Trinidad* and
the whole of the Spanish fleet. The *Captain* might be
crushed or sunk,—taken, he knew, she could not be ;
but whatever happened to her, he ensured sufficient
delay to permit the *Culloden, Blenheim, Prince George,
Orion,* and others to come up. To see and understand
this, however, required some knowledge of ships and
fleets and naval tactics ; while the most ignorant could
see and understand the grandeur of one ship capturing
two others, each bigger than herself, and were pleased
to represent Nelson as a man whose one idea of a battle

was to plunge blindfold into the thickest of it, trusting to the fortune of war to bring him well out of it.

Much has been written of the very inadequate account of the battle and of Nelson's share in it which was given in Jervis's despatch. It may be that, as has been said, there was some jealousy on the part of Sir Robert Calder, the Captain of the Fleet; but Jervis was not the man to be guided by a Calder, or by any one else, in a way that his own judgment did not approve; and it may very well be that he considered it unbecoming to enter into the details of the battle in his public letter. It had certainly not been usual to do so. In a private letter to the First Lord he rendered full justice to Nelson's gallantry, though still without entering into any detail; and in all probability Lord Spencer first learned what was actually done from Sir Gilbert Elliot, who had witnessed the battle from the deck of the *Lively* frigate, which after the battle carried him and Calder and the Admiral's despatches to England.

Rewards and promotions were showered on the victors. Jervis, who had previously been notified of the King's intention to raise him to the peerage as a baron, was now made an earl, the King himself suggesting the title of St. Vincent. Nelson received the freedom of the City of London in a gold casket and a sword of honour. The city of Norwich also conferred its freedom, at once as a recognition of his valour and in return for the Spanish Rear-Admiral's sword, which he presented to the corporation. By the King he was made a Knight of the Bath, an honour then at least equal, probably superior, in social prestige to the Grand Cross of the present day. A baronetcy would have been conferred on

him, but in conversation with Elliot, Nelson had expressed
a very distinct objection to receiving any hereditary
title which his means would not allow him to keep up ;
and had very plainly suggested that he would much
prefer the order of the Bath.   There is a common im-
pression that his promotion to the rank of rear-admiral
was also a reward for his splendid conduct on St. Valentine's Day.   This is a mistake.   Neither then nor for
nearly a hundred years before was promotion to flag-
rank a reward for conspicuous merit, but, following
certain more or less clearly defined rules of service,
was conferred according to seniority on the list of post-
captains.   Nelson, a captain of more than seventeen
years' standing, had been close to the top of the list for
several months, and for more than a year had been
apprehensive that his promotion, which must come with
the first batch, would put him on half-pay.   Now, when
it did come, it was dated only six days after the battle,
a fortnight before the news reached England.

After refitting at Lisbon, Nelson, with his broad
pennant still in the *Irresistible*, was sent with a small
squadron to cruise between Cape St. Vincent and the
African coast, on the look-out for the Viceroy of Mexico,
who was expected to arrive at Cadiz with three ships of
the line and a large treasure.   Nelson, writing to his
wife as he put to sea, said : "The Spanish war will give
us a cottage and a piece of ground, which is all I want.
I shall come one day or other laughing back, when we
will retire from the busy scenes of life : I do not,
however, intend to be a hermit ; the dons will give us a
little money."   His anticipations were not, however, to
be fulfilled this cruise, for either the report was un-

founded, or the Viceroy, having intelligence of the war, postponed his departure. On March 24th he again shifted his broad pennant to the *Captain*, which had re-fitted at Lisbon ; and on the afternoon of April 1st he was joined by the Admiral and the fleet. They brought him the news of his promotion to the rank of rear-admiral, and the same afternoon, at three o'clock, he hoisted his flag on board the *Captain*.

For a fortnight longer Nelson continued off Cadiz, and was then again sent to bring away the troops from Porto Ferrajo, if indeed they were not already on the way under the escort of the *Inconstant*. He had previously suggested to the Admiral that the Viceroy might have gone to Teneriffe, and that if so, those soldiers with a detachment of the fleet might capture the island without much difficulty. When, however, he returned to Gibraltar, in company with the convoy which he met near the southern end of Corsica, Jervis, now Earl of St. Vincent, had apparently learnt that the Viceroy had not gone to Teneriffe ; and the troops, being under orders for England, were sent on at once. As it was found necessary for the *Captain* to go to England to be docked, Nelson with Captain Miller moved into the *Theseus*, and resumed the blockade of Cadiz, which was continued for the next two months, enlivened by occasional skirmishes with the Spanish gunboats or launches. In one of these, on July 3rd, Nelson thought that "his personal courage was more conspicuous than at any other period of his life." His barge, containing thirteen men all told, including himself and Fremantle, was boarded by a Spanish gunboat with a crew of thirty, eighteen of whom were killed after a severe hand-to-hand fight, several wounded, and the boat taken. Perhaps the courage which was most conspicuous was that of John Sykes, the coxswain of the barge, who, after parrying several blows meant for Nelson, stopped one with his own head, which was either harder than the run of heads, or the cutlass had turned in the hand; for Sykes, though severely wounded, was not killed till two years later, when a fragment of a bursting cannon found a mortal part.

It was during this time that the Commander-in-Chief was sternly engaged in repressing the mutinous spirit which had shown itself in the fleet. The *Theseus* was supposed to be one of the most deeply infected; it is therefore notable that within three weeks of Nelson's hoisting his flag on board her, a paper professing to be signed by the ship's company was dropped on the quarter-deck:—"Success attend Admiral Nelson! God bless Captain Miller! We thank them for the officers they have placed over us. We are happy and comfortable, and will shed every drop of blood in our veins to support them, and the name of the *Theseus* shall be immortalised as high as the *Captain's*." From that time every appearance of insubordination vanished; and the *Theseus*, which continued under Miller's command till his lamentable death in 1799, was as well disciplined and in as good order as any ship in the fleet.

With the vigorous manner in which Lord St. Vincent stamped out the mutiny then threatening the most dangerous consequences, we are not now concerned. Nelson in the inshore squadron was clear of the trouble; but one expression of his sentiments is of importance as showing how utterly false is the idea that he was a man

to keep things easy by letting those under his command
have their own way. For in fact "the iron grip under
the velvet glove" was never more strikingly illustrated
than in the character of Nelson. Two men of the *St.
George* were tried for mutiny on Saturday, July 8th;
were found guilty, and sentenced to death. St. Vincent
had determined that the sentence, if passed, should be
carried out without delay. The men would have been
hanged on the Saturday, but that the court-martial did
not finish till after sunset; they were actually hanged
at nine o'clock on Sunday morning; whereupon Vice-
Admiral Thompson wrote the Admiral a very strong
letter "censuring him for profaning the Sabbath."
Nelson, on the other hand, wrote : "I congratulate you
on the finish, as it ought, of the *St. George's* business, and
I (if I may be permitted to say so) very much approve
of its being so speedily carried into execution, even
although it is Sunday. The particular situation of the
service requires extraordinary measures. I hope this
will end all the disorders in our fleet: had there been
the same determined spirit at home, I do not believe it
would have been half so bad"; and to the Captain of
the Fleet he added : "I am sorry that you should have
to differ with Vice-Admiral Thompson ; but had it been
Christmas Day instead of Sunday I would have executed
them. We know not what might have been hatched by
a Sunday's grog : now your discipline is safe."

More congenial work was, however, preparing for him.
The Admiral had received intelligence that a richly-
laden ship from Manila had put into Santa Cruz, and was
there waiting for an opportunity to return to Spain.
As Nelson had before suggested the possibility of an

attack on Teneriffe, St. Vincent now recurred to it and proposed to Nelson to carry it out. Nelson readily undertook to do so, though the scheme was no longer his, which had been based on his having the co-operation of a large body of troops. This was now not to be had; and though a squadron of three ships of the line and three frigates was detached for the service, it was found that the attempt was, as Nelson had supposed, impracticable without a much stronger landing-party than they could muster. They were off the Bay of Santa Cruz on July 21st, and as the Governor refused to capitulate, the attack was ordered for the night of the 24th under cover of the darkness. Unfortunately the darkness told against the assailants. Most of the boats missed the mole, and were tossed on shore through a raging surf which stove the boats and wet the ammunition. The few who landed at the mole were exposed to a heavy and well-judged fire. Nelson, in the act of landing, was struck on the right elbow by a grape-shot. He fell back into the arms of his stepson, Josiah Nisbet, at this time a lad of seventeen and lieutenant of the *Theseus*, who took him back to the ship, where the shattered arm was amputated.

On shore the position of the assailants was desperate; and when daylight showed the scanty force of the English surrounded by some eight thousand Spaniards under arms and with five field-pieces, Troubridge, on whom the command devolved, felt it necessary to negotiate. Samuel Hood, Lord Hood's namesake and cousin, a good linguist and at this time captain of the *Zealous*, took a flag of truce and proposed that the Spaniards should find boats and the English should withdraw, pledging themselves to commit no further hostilities. The Governor thought the English ought to surrender as prisoners of war; but Hood replied that Captain Troubridge had directed him to say that if the terms offered were not accepted in five minutes, he would set the town on fire and attack the Spaniards at the point of the bayonet. The Spanish force was presumably in great part a pretence, local militia without training or courage, and the Governor judged it better to accept the terms than force on a conflict with desperate men. He did more, and with a liberality not unprecedented in our wars with Spain, "directed our wounded men to be received into the hospitals, and all our people to be supplied with the best provisions that could be procured, and made it known that the ships were at liberty to send on shore and purchase whatever refreshments they were in want of during the time they might lie off the island." On the 27th, the officers and men were all brought on board, and the squadron, already under way, made sail to rejoin the Admiral.

It was the same day, that is, within about sixty hours from the time of his arm being amputated, that Nelson wrote to Lord St. Vincent,—a few lines only, interesting as his first attempt with his left hand—asking that his stepson might be promoted in the vacancy caused by the death, at Santa Cruz, of Captain Bowen of the *Terpsichore*. As the boy was at this time barely seventeen, the practical elasticity of the rule laid down in the Instructions, that no one should be made a lieutenant till he was twenty, is proved by the facts that Nelson did not see any impropriety in asking that this boy, already a lieutenant, should be made a commander;

and that St. Vincent, in many ways the embodiment
of strict service, saw no impropriety in granting the
request, and promoting the boy to be commander of the
Dolphin hospital-ship.   At the same time he ordered the
Seahorse, whose captain, Fremantle, moved into her from
the *Inconstant*, had also been wounded at Teneriffe, to
take Nelson to England.   The *Theseus* joined the Admiral
off Cadiz on August 16th, when Nelson wrote : " A left-
handed admiral will never again be considered as useful,
therefore the sooner I get to a very humble cottage the
better, and make room for a better man to serve the
State " ; and the next day the *Seahorse* sailed for Spithead, where she anchored on September 1st.

Nelson went at once to Bath, where his wife already
was ; and for several weeks there, or afterward in London,
suffered intense agony from his wound.   It appears that
in the hurry and in the murky atmosphere of the *Theseus's*
cockpit the surgeon had tied a nerve with the artery ;
as the result of which the pain was often extreme, till
in due time the ligature came away ; and even then the
suffering left a neuralgic disposition, the ill effects of
which were never removed.   The story is told that when
the news of Duncan's victory at Camperdown, won on
October 11th, reached London, Nelson was occupying
apartments in Bond Street.   He had been in great pain
all day, and had gone to bed after taking a dose of
laudanum, when the mob, surging through the street,
knocked angrily at the door to ask why the house was
not illuminated.   The servant told them that Sir Horatio
Nelson was there, badly wounded and trying to sleep.
Already his was a name to conjure with.   " You will
hear no more of us," replied the spokesmen of the party ;

and we are left to believe that they took measures to prevent any further disturbance in that quarter. By December 8th Nelson was able to send to the incumbent of St. George's, Hanover Square, this notice, to be used on the following Sunday : "An officer desires to return thanks to Almighty God for his perfect recovery from a severe wound, and also for the many mercies bestowed upon him."

Some weeks before this he had found out that the Admiralty did not consider a left-handed admiral necessarily useless, especially when he was the popular hero of St. Valentine's Day. It had been already decided that the *Foudroyant*, a fine 80-gun ship, then on the stocks but to be launched in January, should be commissioned in February for his flag, and that her captain should be Berry, the old first lieutenant of the *Agamemnon*, who had been posted for his distinguished valour off Cape St. Vincent. It was afterwards found that the *Foudroyant* could not be ready so soon as had been expected ; and, as the Admiralty were anxious that Nelson should rejoin Lord St. Vincent without delay, and he himself was eager to be afloat again, it was arranged that for the time he should hoist his flag on board the *Vanguard* of 74 guns, Berry going with him as his flag-captain. He sailed from St. Helen's on April 10th, 1798, anchored in the Tagus on the 23rd, and on the last day of the month joined the Commander-in-Chief off Cadiz.

CHAPTER VI

THE BATTLE OF THE NILE

IT was already known that a very considerable French force was being got together at Toulon, though its object or destination remained a secret; and Lord St. Vincent at once determined to send Nelson with a small squadron up the Mediterranean, to try if he could find out anything about it. The rumours were various. Sicily, Corfu, Portugal, and Ireland were all mentioned as its possible aims; it was, perhaps, intended to join a Spanish force at Cartagena. Nelson was instructed to send off a frigate or sloop to the Admiral so soon as he discovered anything; but in any case to take care that the enemy did not pass him, so as to prevent his rejoining the fleet.

With two line-of-battle ships, the *Orion* and *Alexander*, besides the *Vanguard*, three frigates and a sloop, Nelson sailed from Gibraltar on May 8th. Ten days later he wrote from off Cape Sicie that there were in Toulon fifteen sail of the line apparently ready for sea, that there were many transports, and that large bodies of troops were daily arriving at the port; about twelve thousand men were already embarked; the time of sailing was very differently reported; and as to further particulars, — "they order their matters so well in France that all is secret."

The next day, May 18th, it came on to blow; and early on the morning of the 20th the *Vanguard's* masts, —the main topmast, the mizen topmast, the foremast— went over the side one after the other; the bowsprit, badly sprung, and the lower main and mizen masts were all that remained. The gale blew very hard all day, and the *Vanguard* laboured exceedingly. The *Alexander* took her in tow, and the *Orion*, finding the anchorage of San Pietro at the southern end of Sardinia, piloted her in. The three line-of-battle ships anchored there at noon on the 23rd. The frigates and small craft, by stress of weather, had parted company; and not finding their consorts, and concluding that the *Vanguard* would be obliged to return to Gibraltar, went back to the fleet; nor did Nelson see them again during the anxious months that were to follow. In four days, by the united exertions of the three ships, the *Vanguard* was refitted,—a main topmast for a foremast, a top-gallant mast for a topmast, and everything else reduced in proportion — and the squadron again at sea. Four days later it was back off Toulon; but the French fleet was no longer there. The same northerly gale which had proved so disastrous to the *Vanguard*, was, a little to the eastward, a fine fresh breeze, with which the French expedition had put to sea and disappeared. No further information could be obtained, and for some days Nelson vainly sought for it along the coast of Italy, being unwilling to go south without some definite purpose.

Meanwhile the Government, having also heard of this threatening armament at Toulon, had sent out a strong reinforcement to Lord St. Vincent, with instructions to detach a sufficient squadron up the Mediterranean under the command of a "discreet flag officer," suggesting that the fittest for the service would be Sir Horatio Nelson. The suggestion came directly from the First Lord of the Admiralty, who had been prompted by Sir Gilbert Elliot and by the King himself, probably at the request of the Duke of Clarence. St. Vincent's own opinion was quite in accord with the suggestion, and the more so as Nelson was already in the Mediterranean. A squadron of ten 74-gun ships and the 50-gun ship *Leander* was therefore detached under the command of Captain Troubridge, and joined Nelson on the evening of June 7th, bringing him instructions to proceed in quest of the enemy's armament, the object of which was supposed to be either an attack upon Naples and Sicily, the conveyance of an army to some part of the coast of Spain for the purpose of marching towards Portugal, or to pass through the Straits with the view of proceeding to Ireland. On falling in with it, he was to use his utmost endeavours to take, sink, burn, or destroy it; and he was "to remain upon this service so long as the provisions of his squadron would last, or as long as he might be enabled to obtain supplies from any of the ports of the Mediterranean."

Subsequent events give a peculiar and important significance to the wording of this order. It should therefore be especially noticed that he was enjoined to remain so long as he could obtain supplies; to obey this order not only in the letter but in the spirit, by treating as hostile any ports within the Mediterranean where provisions, etc., should be refused; and, definitely and distinctly, to exact supplies of whatever he might be in want of from the territories of the Grand Duke of Tuscany, the King of the Two Sicilies, and others. Nothing can be clearer or more precise than the authority given to Nelson to help himself in case of a refusal; and those have assuredly known little of Nelson's character who have supposed that he would have preferred disobeying his orders and neglecting the special service entrusted to him, to bringing pressure or even force to bear on a doubtful ally. He, however, determined to ascertain at once what he had to depend on; and on June 12th wrote from off Elba to Sir William Hamilton, the English ambassador at Naples, requesting him to assure the King of his determination to support him and also to obtain clear answers to these questions: Are the ports of Naples and Sicily open to His Majesty's fleet? Have the Governors orders for our free admission, and for us to be supplied with whatever we may want? On the 14th he wrote again, to the effect that he had just learned that the French fleet had been seen off Trapani on the 4th; and that if it was now in any port of Sicily, he would at once attack it. He wanted pilots, as well as an answer to his questions. "I send Captain Troubridge to communicate with your Excellency, and, as Captain Troubridge is in full possession of my confidence, I beg that whatever he says may be considered as coming from me."

In a letter to Lord Spencer, dated on the 15th off Ponza, we get the first hint of what was, and no doubt had already been, the dominant idea in his mind,— that the French were aiming at Egypt; an idea the more remarkable as entirely foreign to the instructions or suggestions he had received from the Commander-in-Chief. After saying that they had been seen on the 4th off Trapani steering to the eastward, he went on: "If they pass Sicily, I shall believe they are going on their scheme of possessing Alexandria and getting troops to India, a plan concerted with Tippoo Saib, by no means so difficult as might at first view be imagined; but be they bound to the Antipodes, your lordship may rely that I will not lose a moment in bringing them to action, and endeavour to destroy their transports. I hope," he continued, "the King of Naples will send me some frigates; for mine parted company on May 20th, and have not joined me since. . . . I shall make sail and pass the Faro of Messina the moment Captain Troubridge returns."

Although his first letter to Sir William Hamilton was dated off Elba on June 12th, and the second, introducing Troubridge, off Civita Vecchia on the 14th, the *Mutine* brig, in which Troubridge took a passage, did not part company till the 16th, when she pushed on into the Bay of Naples, anchoring there the next morning while the fleet lay to in the offing. About eight o'clock on the morning of the 17th, Troubridge, accompanied by Hardy, now commander of the *Mutine*, landed and called on Sir William Hamilton, who took him at once to see General Acton, the Neapolitan Prime Minister. Troubridge was much pleased with Acton's answers to his straightforward questions; and on his expressing a desire for an order to the Commanders-in-Chief of all the ports in Sicily to supply the ships with provisions and, in case of an action, to permit them to land the sick and wounded, the General gave him such an order in the name of His Sicilian Majesty, signed by himself and addressed to all the several governors of the different ports in Sicily.   In addition to this order, Troubridge took off a copy of a letter to Hamilton from the Marquis de Gallo, the Neapolitan Foreign Secretary, dated June 12th, to the effect that they could not venture to take a decided part while the treaty with Austria was still unsettled, and in view of the possibility of the withdrawal of the English fleet; but that by the King's express orders the English squadron would receive every welcome, facility and advantage compatible with the circumstances. He was also able to give Nelson the information that the French fleet had passed Sicily and was attacking Malta; with news from Pantellaria that a French ship had been making inquiries there relative to the report of a British squadron's being in the Mediterranean, which they thought could not be true.   In Sicily they had asked the same, and been told that for two years British colours had not been seen there, except on board some Gibraltar privateers.

Hoping to catch the French fleet unawares before Malta, Nelson made sail at once, and passed through the Strait of Messina, writing to Hamilton on the next day, June 18th, that the Cabinet was determined to keep the fleet in the Mediterranean, and that he might assure the King of Naples that he should not withdraw but by positive orders or the impossibility of procuring supplies.   His letter concluded with a complimentary message to Lady Hamilton, and the expression of a hope to be presented to her " crowned with laurel or cypress," referring, with a strange misappropriation of language, to the speech of Opdam as he sailed to the battle of June 4th, 1665.

Off Cape Passaro, on the 22nd, Nelson learned that Malta had tamely surrendered to the French on the 15th, and that on the 16th the whole fleet, consisting of sixteen sail of the line, with frigates, bombs, etc., and near three hundred transports, had left the island. As Sicily was not their object, and as, from the time they sailed, the wind blew fresh from the west, Nelson judged that their destination was eastward, and was convinced that their object was to possess themselves of some port in Egypt and to fix themselves at the head of the Red Sea, in order to get a formidable army into India. And thus, without any direct intelligence but strong in his conviction, and assured by learning from Troubridge that it was shared by Hamilton and Acton, he sailed for Alexandria, hoping to come across the French fleet on the way, but beginning to think, as days passed and he saw nothing of them, that they must have heard from Naples of the approach of an English fleet and have turned aside, perhaps to Corfu.

When, therefore, he arrived off Alexandria, and found that the French were neither there nor had been heard of, he at once reverted to the other idea, and imagined that they must have turned up the Adriatic or the Archipelago, or had perhaps kept a more northerly course and were hugging the Syrian coast. Wherever they were, it was his business to find them; and sailing northwards, he searched along the coast of Syria and then along the coast of Caramania; but neither by sight nor inquiry could he learn anything of the French fleet.

It was now getting towards the end of July, nearly

three months since he had left the Admiral. The water
was beginning to run short, and the men to need fresh
provisions. Relying therefore on the order which he had
received from Acton, and empowered to use force if
necessary, he made straight for Syracuse, and on the
afternoon of the 19th ran into the harbour, anchored,
moored, and sent the boats on shore for water,—all without paying any attention to the Governor's remonstrances
beyond forwarding him Acton's letter. The Governor
was in some doubt how far this, irregular in form and
wanting in precision, warranted him in permitting such
a flagrant breach of the treaty with France, by the terms
of which not more than four foreign ships of war were
to be admitted at one time to any Neapolitan port. He
realised, however, the utter impossibility of getting rid
of his visitors before their wants were satisfied; as the
town lay exposed to their broadsides, force was clearly
out of the question; and so, salving his conscience with
continued remonstrances, which seem to have put Nelson
in a very bad temper, he sanctioned an unrestrained
trade in fruit and vegetables, bullocks, and wine, as well
as, under the rose, in *acquarzente*, if we may judge by
the number of men in the fleet who were flogged for
drunkenness during the short stay.

The squadron left Syracuse on July 25th; on the 28th,
being off the Gulf of Coron, Nelson learned that the
French fleet had been seen about four weeks before,
steering towards the south-east from Candia; and satisfied that, after all, they had gone to Egypt, he at once
made sail for Alexandria. On the evening of the 31st,
as he was nearing that port, he sent the *Alexander* and
Swiftsure ahead to reconnoitre; but at noon on August 1st,

being in sight of Alexandria and seeing that, while the harbour was full of transports, the men - of - war were not there, he altered course to the eastward. A little before three the *Zealous* signalled that she saw sixteen sail of the line at anchor ; they were, in fact, thirteen sail of the line and four large frigates lying close in-shore in Aboukir Bay.

During the many weeks that he had been groping for this fleet, Nelson had had frequent opportunities of explaining to the several captains with him the plan on which he meant to engage at sea or at anchor ; and now, as they saw the enemy before them, very few signals were sufficient to let them know what they had to do. The wind was variable from north-west to north-north-west, and the French fleet was moored in a broken line following very closely the five-fathom line of soundings, about three miles from the shore ; so that while the general direction of their line was from north-west to south-east, that of the van was really from about west-north-west to east-south-east, and of the rear from about north-north-west to south-south-east. It would thus seem as if the van of the French fleet was in a bow and quarter line rather than in line ahead, and it has been so described by some writers who have not noticed that, in preparing for action, the French ships got into line ahead, either by putting springs on their cables or letting fall another anchor. But the general effect was that their line was approximately in the line of the wind; and as Nelson drew near enough to understand the position, he signalled that it was his intention to attack the enemy's van and centre. It was then nearly five o'clock. He had previously made the signal to prepare to anchor by the stern with springs on the cables; and a little before six he made the signal to form line of battle as most convenient, ahead and astern of the Admiral. He had with him at the moment only ten ships of 74 guns; the *Culloden*, which had been towing a small prize laden with wine, was some miles astern; and still farther astern were the *Alexander* and *Swiftsure*, with the little *Leander*.

And now, before the battle begins, it may be well to say a few words as to the relative force of the two fleets. With the exception of the *Leander*, the English ships were all of 74 guns, of the smaller class, carrying 32-pounders on the lower deck and 18-pounders on the main or, as it was then called, the upper deck; the *Leander* had 24 and 12 pounders respectively. Most of them had been for upwards of a year in commission, many of them for upwards of two years, and under the iron rule of Jervis had been brought into a state of the greatest efficiency. The following is a list of them in the order they got into as they formed line of battle, the order in which they went into action. The *Culloden*, attempting a short cut, struck on a rock at the eastern end of the shoal running out from Aboukir, or, as it has since been called, Nelson Island, remained fast, and had no part in the fight.

	Ships' Names.	Captains.	Men.	K.	W.	Total.
1	*Goliath* . .	Thomas Foley	590	21	41	62
2	*Zealous* . .	Sam. Hood	590	1	7	8
3	*Orion* . .	Sir J. Saumarez	590	13	29	42
4	*Audacious* .	Davidge Gould	590	1	35	36
5	*Theseus* . .	R. W. Miller	590	5	30	35
6	*Vanguard* .	R.-Adml. Sir H. Nelson Ed. Berry	595	30	75	105
7	*Minotaur* .	Thomas Louis	640	23	64	87
8	*Defence* . .	John Peyton	590	4	11	15
9	*Bellerophon*	H. d'E. Darby	590	49	148	197
10	*Majestic* . .	G. B. Westcott	590	50	143	193
11	*Swiftsure* .	Ben. Hallowell	590	7	22	29
12	*Alexander* .	A. J. Ball	590	14	58	72
13	*Leander* . .	T. B. Thompson	343	0	14	14
14	*Culloden* .	T. Troubridge	...	...	...	...

In nominal force the French were far superior, as appears from the following list, in which the ships are numbered from the van or north-west, to the rear or south-east.

	Ships' Names.	Guns.	Men.	Result of the Battle.
1	*Guerrier*	74	700	Taken
2	*Conquérant*	74	700	Taken
3	*Spartiate*	74	700	Taken
4	*Aquilon*	74	700	Taken
5	*Peuple Souverain* . .	74	700	Taken
6	*Franklin*	80	800	Taken
7	*Orient*	120	1010	Blown up
8	*Tonnant*	80	800	Taken
9	*Heureux*	74	700	Taken
10	*Mercure*	74	700	Taken
11	*Guillaume Tell* . .	80	800	Escaped
12	*Généreux*	74	700	Escaped
13	*Timoleon*	74	700	Burnt
14	*Sérieuse*	36	300	Sunk
15	*Artemise*	36	300	Burnt
16	*Diane*	40	400	Escaped
17	*Justice*	40	400	Escaped

When we remember that in tonnage and weight of metal a French 74-gun ship was greater by one-fifth than an English, that a French 80-gun ship was, in the same way, greater than an English 74 by one third, and that the 120-gun ship was equal to two English 74's, the superiority of the French will appear very marked. It was, however, more apparent than real. Notwithstanding the fashion of the present day, our forefathers were never convinced that 40-pounders were a more efficient armament than 32's, and believed that they could not be worked so quickly even with a much greater number of men. But independently of this, many of the French ships were old; some were barely seaworthy, and could only carry a reduced armament. The *Conquérant* is said to have had only 18 and 12 pounders on her lower and main decks respectively. The *Guerrier* and *Peuple Souverain* had been condemned the previous year. The men, too, were newly raised. Many of them were not seamen; they had not been trained to the exercise of the guns; they were in a bad state of discipline; and their numbers are said to have been far below the established complements, the deficiency while the fleet was at sea being filled up with soldiers who landed with the army of invasion. French writers have also laid stress on the fact that when the English were first sighted, their boats were on shore watering. But as that was about two o'clock in the afternoon, as the boats were at once recalled, and as the action did not begin till near seven, it is difficult to see that the circumstance had that importance which has been attributed to it. On the other hand, many men had certainly been drafted from the transports and storeships at Alexandria;

and, at the last moment, the greater part of the frigates' crews were distributed among the ships of the line of battle ; so that, in all probability, the numbers actually on board were not much short of the establishment, and were beyond doubt considerably greater than those of the English.

As the headmost ships of the English line drew near, the French opened on them a fire which, from their position nearly end on, they were unable to return ; nor was it intended they should do so. But about twenty minutes to seven, the *Goliath*, passing across the bows of the *Guerrier*, barely clearing her jib-boom, poured in a terrific broadside, and rounding to, let go her stern anchor abreast, but inshore of the French ship. She had, however, too much way on, and only brought up abreast of the *Conquérant*. Her place was immediately taken by the *Zealous*, after she also had discharged her broadside into the *Guerrier's* bow. The *Orion*, following, passed inshore of the *Zealous* and *Goliath*, ran foul of the *Sérieuse*, which, disabled by the shock, drifted on to the shore in a sinking state, and anchored abreast of the *Peuple Souverain*. Like the others, the *Theseus*, — every gun loaded with two, some with three, round-shot,—reserved her fire till she had the *Guerrier's* masts in a line, with the jib-boom about six feet clear of her own rigging. Her broadside brought down the *Guerrier's* masts ; and then, passing between her and the *Zealous*, and as close as possible on the offside of the *Goliath*, she anchored abreast of the *Spartiate*. The *Audacious* passed between the *Guerrier* and the *Conquérant*, pouring a raking broadside into each, and let go her anchor close on the *Conquérant's* inner bow. These five ships thus all passed inside ; all, as they did so, raked the enemy with terrible effect, and were all clustered about the headmost ships of the French line.

The sixth ship, the *Vanguard*, with Nelson's flag at the mizen, anchored by the stern, outside and abreast of the *Spartiate*. The other ships followed, the *Minotaur* anchoring abreast of the *Aquilon*, the *Defence* abreast of the *Peuple Souverain*. The *Bellerophon* let go her anchor on the starboard bow of the *Orient*, but, having too much way on, did not bring up till she had opened the three-decker's broadside, and became singly opposed to the fire of that enormous ship before her own broadside completely bore. She thus sustained very great loss, and cutting her cable, drifted along the French line and anchored again some distance to the eastward, where she remained till the next day with her ensign flying on the stump of her main-mast, her captain wounded, and three of her lieutenants killed. The *Majestic* fared nearly as badly ; whether on account of the darkness and smoke, or, as in the other cases, from her anchor not bringing her up, she ran her jib-boom into the main-rigging of the *Heureux*, and remained in that position for some time, suffering greatly. Her main and mizen masts went by the board ; her captain was killed by a musket-ball through the neck. At length she disentangled herself, and bringing her broadside to bear on the starboard bow of the *Mercure*, took a severe revenge. The *Swift-sure* and *Alexander*, warned off from the dangerous shoal by the fate of the *Culloden*, came into action a few minutes past eight, and anchored, one on each bow of the *Orient*. An hour later the *Leander*, which had waited to offer assistance to the *Culloden*, anchored in comparative safety athwart the hawse of the *Franklin*.

By this time the five headmost ships of the French line were completely subdued. A little before ten, the *Orient* caught fire on the poop, probably, as was supposed, by the ignition of some carcasses or inflammable composition she had on board. The furious cannonade from the guns of the *Swiftsure* and *Alexander* directed towards the spot prevented all attempts to extinguish the flames, and the ship was soon in a blaze; about half-past ten she blew up, the explosion and the fall of the burning wreck causing imminent danger to the English ships near, especially to the *Alexander* which was on fire in several places. The victory was now assured; and though towards morning the action was partially renewed in the rear, further resistance was but slight. The *Guillaume Tell* and the *Généreux*, with the frigates *Justice* and *Diane*, fled; the *Timoléon*, endeavouring to follow them, was driven on shore, where, the next day, her crew set her on fire and escaped to the land.

Never in the annals of modern war had a victory been so complete. Nelson thought that it would have been still more so, that the *Guillaume Tell* and the *Généreux* would also have been taken, had he not been incapacitated by a wound in the head. This was, perhaps, mere fancy, and differs from his official statement to Lord St. Vincent, which ran: "These two ships, with two frigates, I am sorry to say, made their escape, nor was it in my power to prevent them. Captain Hood most handsomely endeavoured to do it, but I had no ship in a condition to support the *Zealous*, and I was obliged to call her in." Berry's narrative, written with a knowledge of the Admiral's despatch, almost repeats its words ; but Captain Miller, writing to his wife independently and privately, said : " The Admiral made the *Zealous, Goliath, Audacious,* and *Leander* signals to chase the others ; the *Zealous* very gallantly pushed at them alone, and exchanged broadsides as she passed close on the different tacks ; but they had so much the start of the other ships and now of the *Zealous,* who had suffered much in her rigging, and knowing also they were remarkably fast sailers, the Admiral made the general signal of recall, and these four ships were soon out of sight." It is not easy to see what more could have been done, even if the Admiral had not been wounded. As it was, the wound, though severe and at first considered dangerous, did not by any means disable him. He was struck on the forehead by a piece of langridge, which cut a large flap of skin and flesh ; and this, falling over his eye, and with the gush of blood, completely blinded him for the moment. When, however, the blood was stanched and the wound dressed, he was able to come on deck, watch the *Orient* blow up, and order boats to be sent to pick up her men. Whether he was actually on deck on the morning of the 2nd does not appear ; most probably he was, though later in the day he permitted himself to be put to bed.

The principle on which the battle was fought is so clear that further explanation is needless ; and we have Berry's distinct assurance that everything went exactly as it had been arranged, and that Nelson's plan was minutely and precisely executed. Unless we suppose Berry to have been guilty of saying the thing that was not, and that he knew was not, this completely disposes of the attempt which has been made to attribute the design of passing inside the French line to Captain Foley of the *Goliath*. It is, indeed, quite possible that the anchoring inside or outside was left to the judgment of the captain of the leading ship ; but independent of Berry's authoritative statement, we may be very sure that Nelson, in discussing and explaining the various situations, spoke of the probability of the enemy not clearing for action on the offside. After being in Hood's confidence, it is incredible that he did not know that the French had committed this blunder when they met Rodney to leeward of Dominica in April, 1782, and did not calculate on their repeating it,—as, in fact, they did.

From beginning to end the plan of the attack bears marks of Hood's teaching, though Hood himself had never been able to put it in practice. But, tracing the idea a little farther back, it is very probable that Hood's thoughts had first been directed to it by Captain John Elphinston, who, while serving as an admiral in the Russian service, had proposed a similar method for the attack on the Turks at Chesme in 1770, although he too had been prevented from carrying it out. What is of more importance, as marking the genius of the man who now worked out to a successful issue a design which had only been proposed by his very able predecessors, is the fact, which French writers have systematically lost sight of, that throughout the century, and especially during the war of American Independence, French naval commanders had, by their persistent practice, shown their belief that a fleet moored in line of battle, with its extremities protected by batteries on shore, was virtually unassailable. Later French writers have repeatedly

accused their admiral, Brueys, of fatuous ineptitude for
lying with his fleet in an exposed roadstead, contrary to
the directions of Bonaparte, and knowing that a superior
English fleet was in the neighbourhood.   As to which
last, it does not appear that either Brueys or Bonaparte
had any knowledge whatever of an English fleet being
within the Mediterranean; and even if Brueys had
known of it, he might very well be excused for believing
that it was not superior; the conduct of the English
fleet under Hotham had not been such as to convince
the southern Frenchmen of their inferiority.

The point of greater interest is the blame that has
been assigned to Brueys for neglecting the General's
order to go inside the harbour of Alexandria.   It is
unnecessary to discuss what would have happened to
the French fleet had Nelson found it there.   As it was,
he wrote that, if he had had some bomb-vessels, "In
forty-eight hours after the victory every transport and
all the stores in them would have been destroyed at
Alexandria; for the port is so very small and so crowded
that not one shell or carcass could have fell amiss."
That the French fleet, if in the harbour, would have
been kept there till bomb-vessels arrived, may be considered certain; and Brueys was quite able to understand that, if Bonaparte was not.   French writers, wise
after the event, have dwelt on the obvious insecurity of
the position in Aboukir Bay: they have lost sight of the
fact that D'Estaing, whom they delight to speak of as a
man of ebullient courage, did, on two separate occasions,
refuse to attack a very inferior English fleet at anchor;
and on a third occasion, when he did attack, suffered
himself to be ignominiously beaten off.   It is said, and

is probably true, that on this occasion, at St. Lucia, Suffren, then captain of the *Fantasque*, implored him to go in and anchor on the enemy's buoys, when the batteries would be neutralised, and he would be able to crush the squadron by superior force. As he had twelve large ships, of 74 or 80 guns, against seven small ones, of 50 or 64 guns, it is impossible to doubt that Barrington would have been in a very awkward predicament if D'Estaing could have mustered sufficient resolution to follow Suffren's advice. With such odds in his favour, he had nothing to do but go in and win ; but this was just what the unwritten law of French tactics absolutely forbade.

For it was not only D'Estaing, of ebullient courage, who manifested this reluctance to attack a fleet anchored in line of battle. In August, 1781, when the combined fleet of thirty-six sail of the line under Cordova and Guichen entered the Channel, they judged it imprudent to attack Darby, who with twenty ships took up a position in Torbay ; and in January, 1782, when Hood anchored off the Basse-terre of St. Kitts, entirely unsupported by batteries on shore, De Grasse, stung into attacking him, did so in the same desultory manner and with as little success as D'Estaing at St. Lucia. It is unnecessary to mention further instances of the French practice ; but it was of perhaps equal importance that, on two occasions, Hood had had an apparent opportunity of attacking a French fleet at anchor and had not availed himself of it, although on one of them, in Golfe Jouan, he had had an overwhelming superiority of force. We know now that both at St. Kitts and in Golfe Jouan Hood had intended to attack, and was only prevented from doing so by accidental circumstances; but the French did not know it, and may be excused for believing that he considered it imprudent even to attempt it.

The French based their belief on the experience of more than a hundred years, and Nelson had not then shown them that it was altogether fallacious. In this respect modern critics have the advantage over Admiral Brueys, as appears indeed, among many other indications, from his firm idea that if any attack was made, it would be on the rear, that is, on the end out of range of the guns and mortars on Aboukir Island. But he did not survive to give his explanations; he was cut in two by a round-shot some time before the *Orient* blew up, and has ever since been the mark of false accusations and false criticism. He was not a man of brilliant genius, but seems to have been a good and brave officer. So also was his chief of the staff, Casabianca, who, with his young son, perished in the explosion, not exactly in the way described in Mrs. Hemans's popular little poem.

On August 2nd, so soon as the action was finished by the flight of the *Guillaume Tell* and *Généreux* and the running ashore of the *Timoléon*, Nelson issued the general order : " Almighty God having blessed His Majesty's arms with victory, the Admiral intends returning public thanksgiving for the same at two o'clock this day, and he recommends every ship doing the same as soon as convenient." This he signed himself, as also a letter of thanks and congratulations to the captains, officers, seamen, and marines of the squadron, an acting-order to the first-lieutenant of the *Majestic* to command her in the room of Captain Westcott, and an order to Berry to go on board the *Leander* with the despatches to Lord St.

Vincent. Wounded as he was, he still gave his attention to the many details of the service which Berry might very well have done for him, or which might have waited. The despatch to St. Vincent, for instance, was dated on the 3rd, and the *Leander* did not sail till the 6th; so that there was no pressing necessity for the order to Berry on the 2nd. But it is probable that the fever induced by the wound caused an abnormal excitement of the brain, which it was considered safer to humour than to check altogether. If the man would not rest, he might busy himself about trifles. On the 3rd he was able to write a holograph letter to Sir James Saumarez and the several captains of the fleet, thanking them for the sword they offered him, and promising, in accordance with their request, to have his portrait painted on the first opportunity, "to be hung up in the room belonging to the Egyptian Club, now established in commemoration of that glorious day," August 1st. It seems doubtful whether the establishment of the Club went any farther than the subscription for the sword; and though many portraits of Nelson were painted both at Naples and in England, there is no record of any one having been appropriated in the promised manner.

The *Leander*, which, with Berry and the despatches for the Commander-in-Chief on board, sailed for the fleet on August 6th, fell in with the *Généreux* on the coast of Candia on the 18th, and after an obstinate defence, in which Berry was severely wounded, was captured. She was taken to Corfu, whence her officers and men, after being very rudely treated and robbed even of their clothes, were sent on to Trieste and released on their parole. It was the beginning of December before Berry arrived in England. But meanwhile Nelson had sent Captain Capel (the Hon. Thomas Bladen Capel, just promoted to the command of the *Mutine*) to Naples, to carry a copy of his despatch overland to the Admiralty.

The *Mutine* reached Naples on September 1st, when the news threw the Neapolitans into the wildest excitement. Their Government had been very anxious lest the French expedition, evading or defeating the English fleet, should return to wreak on them its vengeance for the broken treaty and the alliance with Austria. Now that the French fleet was destroyed and the French army shut up in Egypt, they felt safe; and still more, they felt the delight of knowing that those who had terrified them were themselves crushed and humbled. Everybody, from the Queen to the poorest beggar, was, or pretended to be, in a frenzy of joy; and the most frenzied among them was Lady Hamilton, the wife of the English ambassador, whom circumstances had associated in a very intimate manner with the fortunes of the Queen, and who now drove about Naples in an open carriage, with a bandeau on her head bearing the legend, NELSON AND VICTORY. But all the English in Naples were wildly enthusiastic; and Sir William Hamilton, meeting the Cardinal of York in the street, stopped his carriage to tell him the news. The Prince, to whom Sir William was unknown, seemed at first to resent the liberty; but on hearing what he had to say, answered that he never could forget that he was English, and that he shared in the joy which all Englishmen must feel at so glorious a victory.

When Capel brought the news to London on October

2nd, the enthusiasm, though not so wild, nor so theatrical, was perhaps more real. The very next day, October 3rd, the City of London voted two hundred guineas for a sword of honour for Nelson, and to Berry the freedom of the City in a gold box of the value of one hundred guineas. On the 6th Nelson was gazetted a peer by the title of Baron Nelson of the Nile and Burnham Thorpe. On Sunday the 21st and on the two following Sundays, a special thanksgiving prayer for the victory was read in all the churches, including, of course, those of Burnham Thorpe and Hilborough. Parliament met on November 20th, when the King's speech specially referred to the "great and brilliant victory" as "a blow to the power and influence of France, affording an opening which, if improved by suitable exertions on the part of other Powers, may lead to the general deliverance of Europe." On the 21st the two Houses of Parliament unanimously passed votes of thanks to Nelson, to the captains and officers, and to the seamen and marines of the fleet; on the 22nd the House of Commons addressed the King, praying him to give directions for a monument in St. Paul's to the memory of Captain Westcott; and on the 23rd, voted a pension of £2000 per annum to Nelson and the two next heirs to the title. A gold medal was ordered for Nelson and all the captains of ships of the line. The Emperor of Russia sent the victorious Admiral a gold box set with diamonds; the Sultan of Turkey sent a diamond aigrette, or "Plume of Triumph," taken from one of the imperial turbans; the Sultan's mother sent a box set with diamonds valued at £1000. From the King of Naples he received a sword of honour; from the King of Sardinia a box set with diamonds; from the East India Company £10,000; from the Turkey Company a piece of plate; and £500 for a piece of plate from the Patriotic Fund; besides the freedom of very many corporations.

From his many friends and acquaintances,—the Duke of Clarence, Lord Hood, Captain Locker, Lady Parker, among others—Nelson received letters of warm congratulation; and one from Lord Howe, to whom he was personally unknown, but who trusted he would "forgive the additional trouble of my compliments on this singular occasion, not less memorable for the skill than cool judgment testified under the considerable disadvantages in the superior force and situation of the enemy." In acknowledging this letter in the following January, Nelson expressed the high value which he placed on the "approbation of the great, the immortal Earl Howe—an honour the most flattering a sea-officer could receive, as it comes from the first and greatest sea-officer the world has ever produced." Nelson's reply is, however, most notable for its brief exposition of the plan on which the battle was fought, an exposition sufficient in itself to demolish the popular theory that the chief characteristic of his genius was his courage; that he won victories by the directness and impetuosity of his attack; that his one idea of tactics was "go at 'em"; and that fortune favoured the brave.

The more closely Nelson's actions and letters are studied, the more clearly will it be seen that the point on which his thoughts continually dwelt was not the mere "going at 'em," but the most advantageous way to "go at 'em"; and that, in every instance, the dash and impetuosity which caught the popular fancy were guided by genius, and controlled by prudence and foresight. On this occasion he wrote: "By attacking the enemy's van and centre, the wind blowing directly along their line, I was enabled to throw what force I pleased on a few ships. This plan my friends readily conceived by the signals, and we always kept a superior force to the enemy. . . . I have never before detailed the action to any one, but I should have thought it wrong to have kept it from one who is our great master in naval tactics and bravery."

After refitting such of the prizes as were at all sea-worthy, they were sent to Gibraltar with the greater part of the squadron under the command of Sir James Saumarez. The other prizes were burned; the *Culloden* and *Alexander* were sent to Naples to refit, and Nelson in the *Vanguard* followed them, leaving Hood in the *Zealous* to keep up the blockade of Alexandria.

CHAPTER VII

THE arrival of the *Vanguard* in Naples Bay on September 22nd was the signal for a fresh outburst of public joy, Lady Hamilton again making herself conspicuous by her impassioned demonstration. As the ship anchored, she, accompanied by her husband, was the first to go on board, and exclaiming, "O God, is it possible!" fell fainting on Nelson's arm. A burst of tears relieved her, and she was quite recovered before the King came on board and, taking Nelson by the hand, hailed him as his " Deliverer and Preserver."

This was practically the beginning of Nelson's acquaintance with Lady Hamilton ; for though he had met her during his short visit to Naples five years before, and though in his occasional letters to her husband he had generally added some courteous message for her, it was now for the first time that he was thrown into her society in circumstances which at once established an intimacy destined to have a marked influence on Nelson's fortunes.

Though now the wife of the English ambassador, received in the best Neapolitan Society and the *confidante* of the Queen, Lady Hamilton was a woman of very humble origin and disreputable antecedents. Amy Lyon, the daughter of a village blacksmith in Cheshire, was born probably in 1761, and when about seventeen came up to London as a domestic servant, a respectable position which she did not long retain. She was of remarkable beauty and giddy disposition, and threw herself into the whirl of pleasure and dissipation. After several *liaisons* of longer or shorter duration, she became the mistress of the Hon. Charles Greville, with whom she remained for about four years leading a life of comparative respectability. During this time she made the acquaintance of Romney, who seems to have considered it his chief happiness to paint her portrait. She was painted also by Reynolds, Hoppner, and Lawrence, so that altogether pictures of her in the full flush of her beauty are very common. In 1786 Greville's affairs fell into confusion, and he seems to have had no scruple about proposing to his uncle, Sir William Hamilton, to take the girl off his hands. This Hamilton readily agreed to do ; and accordingly Amy Lyon, or, as at this time she preferred to call herself, Emily Harte, was sent to Naples, where she presently became Hamilton's mistress, and five years later Hamilton's wife.

While she lived with Greville, as afterwards with Hamilton, every attention was paid to improving her education. She sang well ; she spoke Italian fluently, and without the vulgar accent which she never got rid of in speaking English. Her singing, her dancing, her attitudes after the antique, her readiness in conversation and in repartee, made her welcome everywhere, and the Neapolitans did not trouble to inquire too closely into the truth of her hints of a secret marriage. Afterwards, as Hamilton's wife, she was the recognised leader of the English society. She was lively, clever, unaffected, good-humoured, and withal exceedingly beautiful, although as years crept on her figure lost its delicate proportions. As early as 1796 Sir Gilbert Elliot described her as "monstrous," and ten years later the caricatures represented her as of enormous bulk.

When the atrocities of the French Revolution and the death of Marie-Antoinette rendered the Queen of Naples bitterly hostile to France, she found in Lady Hamilton a convenient medium for secret correspondence with the English ambassador and the English Government; and as Emma, the name she finally determined on, was unquestionably a clever, capable woman, she was trusted with many delicate and confidential matters both by her husband and the Queen. She thus began to consider herself a very important person, and in after years came to believe that she had been the prime motor of the Neapolitan policy at this time. She did not, perhaps, tell lies consciously and intentionally, but her delusion became so complete that she did lie with a very remarkable persistence and thoroughness. Of her many statements as to public affairs there is not one that is not absolutely and entirely untrue. It is, however, only lately that this has been established beyond question; so that for nearly a century she has been represented as a woman who rendered very valuable service to the State at a most critical and difficult period, and who, notwithstanding her faults, was cruelly and shamefully neglected by the government when no longer able to be of use to it.

On Nelson's arrival at Naples, Lady Hamilton virtually took possession of him. Her egregious vanity was
flattered by his open dependence on her, and her real
good-humour was gratified by ministering to his comforts.
The wound on his forehead was healed, but the effects of
the blow still remained. He was subject to violent head-
aches and nervous irritability. The intense strain, too,
of the weeks immediately preceding August 1st had told
on his constitution, already weakened by the suffering
of the previous year. It was a case in which the nurse
was of more use than the physician, and Lady Hamilton
devoted herself to the task. His wife was absent.
She was a good, conscientious woman; too good, too
conscientious, perhaps, to minister to her husband's
weaknesses had she been present. She had nursed him
during his former illness, in dreary lodgings in Bath or
London, and he can scarcely have helped comparing or
contrasting the calm, sedate, perhaps frigid excellence
of Lady Nelson with the vivacity, enthusiasm, and
glowing charms of Lady Hamilton. The difference of
the surroundings, too, was very great. Nelson's income
had always been limited; he had seen little or nothing
of the grandeur and display of the wealthy. His
acquaintance with society scarcely went beyond the
official. No life could be plainer or more frugal than
that which he had led at Burnham Thorpe before he
commissioned the *Agamemnon*. Now everything was
magnificence, splendour, and profusion; the King, the
Queen, the nobles of the Court, Hamilton and all the
English in Naples vying with each other to do him honour.
Festivities, banquets, balls, illuminations dazzled and
enchanted him; and everywhere the central figure

appeared to be his lovely and affectionate nurse, of whose
past history he knew little, and whom he saw on terms
of friendly intimacy with the Queen and the Court. The
rest is a story as old as the myths of Hercules or
Achilles, of all ages and of all climes.

But Nelson, in becoming the slave of a beautiful and
voluptuous woman, did not cease to be a great commander. There is a common idea that his passions
detained him at Naples to the neglect of his duty.
This is erroneous. He made Naples his headquarters
because he was ordered to do so, to provide for the
safety of the kingdom and to take measures for the reduction of Malta. He captured Leghorn : he stationed
such ships as were at his disposal round Malta, under
the immediate command of Captain Ball of the *Alexander*, whose force was strengthened by the arrival of a
small Portuguese squadron under the Marquis de Niza ;
and when the Neapolitan army was ignominiously routed
by the French, who advanced on the capital, he received
the King, with his family and retinue, on board the
Vanguard and the other ships with him at the time, and
conveyed him to Palermo.

The evacuation of Naples was a matter of some
delicacy and difficulty, for the *lazzaroni* were strongly
attached to the King, and broke out into violent and
sanguinary tumult when they suspected that he intended
to leave them. The greatest secrecy was therefore
necessary in making the arrangements which were
planned by the Queen in concert with Nelson, Lady
Hamilton acting as the intermediary and confidential
agent. Many years afterwards it pleased Lady Hamilton
to fancy and assert that she was the moving spirit in the

K

whole business, that she taught the Queen the necessity
of leaving Naples, won her consent, designed the plan
and settled the execution of it, that the King, the Queen,
her husband, and Nelson were but instruments in
her hands. All which, with many imaginative details,
is absolutely untrue. What Nelson wrote at the time,
and assuredly without any wish to depreciate Lady
Hamilton's share in the work, was that, as it would
have been highly imprudent for either Hamilton or
himself to have gone to Court, the correspondence was
carried on with the greatest address by Lady Hamilton
and the Queen, who, being in the habit of interchanging notes, could continue to do so without exciting
suspicion.

For the next few months Nelson remained at
Palermo. The French swept over Italy and occupied
Naples, where the Jacobins received them enthusias-
tically and the people at large made no opposition.
The squadron was dispersed; part of it was off Alexandria, part was blockading Malta, part was protecting
Sicily; it was not till the end of March, 1799, that
a sufficient force for the blockade of Naples could
be got together, and that Troubridge was ordered to
undertake the duty. It was probably about this time
that Nelson was formally appointed Commander-in-
Chief of the Neapolitan navy. The commission itself
cannot now be found, but it appears to be referred to
in a letter to Captain Troubridge of March 30th. "I
herewith enclose you," Nelson wrote, "the final instructions of his Sicilian Majesty, and request you will have
them copied and the originals returned to me; and as
far as lies in your power, to carry them into execution,

always bearing in mind that speedy rewards and quick punishments are the foundation of good government."

At once and without difficulty Troubridge took possession of the several islands on the coast. "The people," he wrote, "are perfectly mad with joy, and are asking for their beloved monarch. If the nobility were men of principle and respectability, how easy it would be to get the Neapolitan soldiers and militia to declare for their King! . . . I beg your Lordship will particularly recommend Captain Chianchi; he is a fine, hardy seaman, a good and loyal subject, desirous of doing everything for the welfare of his country. . . . I have a villain, by name Francesco, on board, who commanded the castle at Ischia, formerly a Neapolitan officer and of property in that island. The moment we took possession of the castle, the mob tore this vagabond's coat, with the tricoloured cape and cap of liberty button, to pieces, and he had then the impudence to put on his Sicilian Majesty's regimentals again; upon which I tore his epaulette off, took his cockade out, and obliged him to throw them overboard. I then honoured him with double irons. . . . I pray your Lordship to send an honest judge here to try these miscreants on the spot, that some proper examples may be made. . . . The villains increase so fast on my hands, and the people are calling for justice; eight or ten of them must be hung."

By the end of April, Salerno, Sorrento, Castellamare, were recovered for the King, and the French, leaving five hundred men to garrison St. Elmo, withdrew to Capua and Caserta. Everywhere the mob was noisily demonstrative in favour of the King, and the great bulk of the people was ready to accept whatever party was in power. Cowardice rather than disaffection seemed the leading factor of the revolution ; but there were many who, from political or selfish motives, had taken an active part in inviting and receiving the French, and others, officers in the King's service, who had betrayed or sold their posts. For such, when they fell into his hands, Troubridge had little pity, and handed them over to the civil power as a matter of course. In one case special orders were given by the King for a court-martial, and Acton, writing of this to Nelson, added : "The King begs and hopes that Captain Troubridge will direct some of his officers to attend to it with the officers of his service, and order accordingly what shall be thought proper at the conclusion of it." Troubridge thought it would be better to leave the court-martial to the Neapolitan officers, but, anticipating a capital sentence, wrote : "If that should be the case, shall I confirm it ? My hand will not shake signing my name. Without some examples, nothing can go well."

It was just at this time, when the reduction of Naples seemed certain, that Nelson received information of the French fleet having escaped from Brest, having probably effected a junction with the Spanish fleet at Cadiz and come into the Mediterranean. He was led to suppose that the combined force might amount to forty-seven sail of the line, and that their first object would be the recovery of Minorca. He at once called in the greater part of his outlying ships from Naples or along the coast and from Malta, with orders to join Rear-Admiral Duckworth off Port Mahon ; but a few days later, conceiving that Sicily was more likely to be their aim, he sent them still more pressing orders to meet him at Marittimo, where he hoped to be joined by Duckworth and, what with Russians, Turks, and Portuguese, to make up a fleet equal in number to the enemy's. He would seem to have learned that the Spaniards had not joined the French.

On quitting Naples, Troubridge left Captain Foote of the *Seahorse* frigate as senior officer to carry on the blockade as closely as possible with the very small squadron at his disposal, and with general instructions to co-operate with Cardinal Ruffo, the commander of the royal forces on shore. Nelson was joined by Troubridge at Palermo on May 17th, but bad weather prevented him sailing till the 20th. On the 23rd he was on the rendezvous off Marittimo ; and having there heard from Lord St. Vincent the actual state of things, he determined to return to Palermo, fill up with provisions, and "hold the squadron in momentary readiness to act as the Commander-in-Chief might order, or the circumstances might require." But he was nervously alive to the possible danger of Sicily if the squadron were to leave it ; so long as the squadron was there in strength, he was convinced that the French would make no attack. What Bruix might have done had leisure been allowed him, it is impossible to say, but the closeness with which he was followed up effectually deranged any plans he had formed ; and eventually he was glad to get out of the Mediterranean and back to Brest without being overtaken by Lord Keith, who at this very critical juncture succeeded St. Vincent as Commander-in-Chief.

On June 13th Nelson had just sailed for Naples, with

troops and stores on board, when he was met by two
74-gun ships detached by Keith with a letter to warn
him of the probability of Bruix coming his way. He
immediately returned to Palermo, disembarked the
troops, and proceeded to his former rendezvous off
Marittimo, where he hoped to be joined by the ships
from Malta. He would then have eighteen sail of the
line, not a three-decker among them, one of them a
64, and three Portuguese, whereas the French had four
first-rates and eighteen or more two-deckers. "I shall
wait off Marittimo," he wrote, "anxiously expecting
such a reinforcement as may enable me to go in search
of the enemy's fleet, when not one moment shall be lost
in bringing them to battle ; for I consider the best
defence for His Sicilian Majesty's dominions is to place
myself alongside the French."

A few days later his intelligence led him to suppose
that the French might be going to Naples. It was
understood that the forts were on the point of surrender-
ing, and that the arrival of the French fleet might leave
the whole work to be done over again. On June 21st
he touched at Palermo, had an interview with the
King, and at once sailed again for Naples, taking with
him Sir William Hamilton and his wife, whose knowledge of Italian might be of the greatest use in confidential communication with Ruffo.

On the way he received intelligence of an armistice
between the King's forces and the rebels. He denounced
it as infamous. To him, as to Troubridge, the rebels
were mutineers and ought to be suppressed ; the idea of
making terms with them was bitterness to him. He
was sure that the arrival of the French fleet would put

an end to the armistice; he determined that the arrival
of the English fleet should equally do so, and as he
entered Naples Bay on the afternoon of the 24th,
signalled the *Seahorse* to haul down the flag of truce.
On anchoring, however, he learned that the armistice
had ended the day before in a capitulation, by the terms
of which the rebels were to be sent to France in vessels
provided by the King. Now it is perfectly well established as the usage of civilised war that terms granted
by a military officer are conditional on the approval of
his superiors, unless he has distinct authority to
negotiate, or the capitulation has been effected wholly
or in part. In the present instance Cardinal Ruffo had
not only no authority to negotiate, but he had express
orders from the King not to do so. Nelson therefore
called the negotiation and the treaty infamous; and
finding that no steps had yet been taken to carry it into
effect, that, in fact, the rebels in the forts were in
exactly the same situation as they were before the
negotiation was commenced, he had no hesitation in
declaring that the treaty was invalid, and that he would
not permit the rebels to embark or quit the forts.
With this resolution he formally acquainted them on
the 25th. "They must," he wrote, "surrender themselves to His Majesty's royal mercy." A copy of this
declaration was sent to the Cardinal, who came on
board the *Foudroyant* to see Nelson about it. A long
and stormy conversation followed, the Hamiltons acting
as interpreters; and at last Nelson wrote that on his
arrival he "found a treaty entered into with the rebels
which, in my opinion, cannot be carried into execution
without the approbation of His Sicilian Majesty." This

he gave to the Cardinal as closing the interview. There can be no doubt that the tenor of this paper was communicated to the garrisons; but even if it was not, the formal declaration sent to them on the 25th was sufficient; and it was with a full knowledge that the treaty was annulled that the forts surrendered to the King's mercy on the evening of the 26th.

With what happened to the prisoners after they were handed over to the civil power Nelson had nothing whatever to do. He knew nothing about them except that they were rebels taken in arms against their sovereign; and with such he had no sympathy. He refused to interfere; he left them to the justice of their country. It may very well be that that justice was not tempered with mercy. The Royalists had been too thoroughly frightened to be in a merciful humour; and assuredly the Jacobins, whether of Italy or France, had not set them an example of clemency. If they had received the same measure as they meted out to others, they would have had small reason for complaint; but in truth the executions, about seventy, with which the Neapolitan Royalists took vengeance for their terror and losses, fade into insignificance when compared with Jacobin enormities.

With one execution only was Nelson in any way concerned. There was a certain Francisco Caracciolo, a man of good family, in the prime of life, a commodore in the Neapolitan navy, who four years before had commanded the *Tancredi* in the fleet under Hotham, and was well esteemed both by his King and the English officers of his acquaintance. This man had accompanied the King and Court to Palermo; but when the Partheno-

peian Republic proclaimed the estates of all absentees to
be forfeited, he obtained leave to go to Naples to arrange
his affairs. The arrangement took the form of his
entering the service of the Republic, of accepting the
post of Admiral of the Republican flotilla, and of commanding the Republican gunboats against a squadron of
the Royal frigates. He had afterwards thrown himself
into one of the Neapolitan sea-forts; but when these
were on the point of capitulating, fearing that he, as a
traitor of the deepest dye, might be exempted, he made
his escape in disguise into the country, where he was
apprehended by some peasants, who brought him on
board the *Foudroyant* in the early morning of June 29th.

Nelson immediately ordered Count Thurn, captain of
the Neapolitan frigate *Minerva*, to assemble a court of
officers of his own service, and try him on a charge of
"rebellion against his lawful sovereign, and for firing at
his colours hoisted on board his frigate, the *Minerva*."
The court was summoned forthwith, and assembled at
nine o'clock the same morning on board the *Foudroyant*.
No objection was made on behalf of the prisoner to the
constitution of the court or to the authority under which
it was convened. His only attempt at defence was an
assertion that he was acting under compulsion; but the
evidence of his being a free agent, and having had
repeated opportunities of escaping had he wished, was
deemed conclusive. He was found guilty, and sentenced
to death. It was then about noon. On receiving the
report, Nelson gave Thurn a detailed order to carry
the sentence into execution without delay; and accordingly Caracciolo was hanged that same evening at the
fore yard-arm of the *Minerva*.

The prompt trial, sentence, and execution of this notorious traitor filled the Italian Jacobins with mingled rage and terror. They sputtered venom and lies, which found their way into print, and were introduced into literature by Southey, whose story was long supposed, and is by many still supposed, to be a faithful narrative of facts. The garrisons, it is said, were taken out of the castles under pretence of carrying the treaty into effect, and were basely delivered over to the vengeance of the Sicilian court. Caracciolo, described as a man of seventy, was, we are told, informally and hurriedly tried by a packed and prejudiced court, summoned without legal authority; and all because the British Admiral was a mere tool in the hands of a foul strumpet bound by interest to a bloodthirsty queen. All of this is absolutely untrue. What actually occurred has been related. Caracciolo was a man of forty-seven, though haggard and worn by misery, privation, and the sense of guilt. With the morality of Lady Hamilton we are not here concerned. With all her faults she was a kindly, soft-hearted woman; but even if she had been the cruel, bloody-minded monster she has been represented, it is sufficiently well attested that she neither spoke to nor saw Nelson between the time of Caracciolo's being brought on board and of his execution. That in cases of mutiny Nelson considered clemency misplaced, and prompt execution advisable, has already been shown; and rebellion such as Caracciolo's was to him the worst form of mutiny. In hanging him the same evening he was strictly following the precedent of St. Vincent's determination off Cadiz only a couple of years before; and to those who carefully consider the circumstances at

Naples, and the pain which this rigid execution of his duty must have given a man of kindly nature, Nelson's conduct at this period, far from being judged blamable, disgraceful, "a stain upon his memory," will appear rather most honourable and meritorious.

Notwithstanding the surrender of the Neapolitan sea-forts the castles Uovo and Nuovo, St. Elmo, which was garrisoned by the French, still held out. Troubridge was ordered to take command of the mixed force on shore, —seamen and marines, Austrians, Russians, Turks, and Neapolitans—and reduce the place without delay. On July 13th Nelson was able to announce its capture, making, at the same time, a particular request that Troubridge's services might be rewarded; consequent on which Troubridge was created a baronet on November 30th.

Nelson's letter had gone but a few hours, when he received an order from Keith to send as many ships to Minorca as he could possibly spare. In a letter to Lord Spencer, just despatched, he had speculated on the probability of his being called on to detach ships for the protection of Minorca. "Should such an order," he wrote, "come at this moment, it would be a cause for some consideration whether Minorca is to be risked, or the two kingdoms of Naples and Sicily. I rather think my decision would be to risk the former." And so it was when the order had actually come. He replied to Keith, in formal language, that the safety of Sicily and Naples required him to stay where he was, and equally prevented him detaching any of his force. To Lord Spencer he wrote more fully and more positively. "I will not part with a single ship," he said. "I am fully aware of the act I have committed; but, sensible of my loyal intentions, I am prepared for any fate which may await my disobedience."

On July 19th he received another and more emphatic order from Keith, dated July 9th; he was to come to Minorca at once with the whole of his force, or if he deemed it absolutely necessary that some part and he himself should remain, he was to detach the greater part under the next senior officer. Nelson again replied, in so many words, that till the French scoundrels should be driven out of the kingdom, "I think it right not to obey your Lordship's order. . . . I have no scruple in deciding that it is better to save the kingdom of Naples and risk Minorca." It was not till July 22nd, when he received a third and still more stringent order to the same effect, that he deemed it expedient to obey, to the extent, at least, of detaching Duckworth with four 74-gun ships; and as Keith left the Mediterranean on the 29th, he heard nothing more about it at the time, though he affected to consider himself ill-treated when, two months later, he received a gentle censure from the Admiralty, accompanied with an order to act as Commander-in-Chief during Keith's absence.

It would thus appear that the Admiralty were willing to allow him a very wide discretion; but the incident has nevertheless a very grave importance, as occurring in the career of a man of such eminence, of one who so constantly laid down the rule that the first duty of an officer is obedience. It does not lessen the crime,—and from the military point of view it was a crime—to say that, after all, Keith was wrong in anticipating an attack on Minorca, and Nelson was probably not wrong in fore-

casting a fresh outbreak if the English squadron was
withdrawn from Naples.   Of the intentions of Bruix
Nelson knew nothing: he believed that Keith was
probably right, and that an attack on Minorca was
pending; but he was of opinion that Naples was of
greater importance than Minorca, and he deliberately
preferred acting on his own opinion to obeying the
orders of the Commander-in-Chief.

It has been frequently alleged that this extraordinary
act of disobedience was prompted by Lady Hamilton in
the interests of the Queen.   There is no evidence that
Lady Hamilton had, directly, anything to do with it;
but it is extremely probable, perhaps almost certain,
that the anxiety which, during all this year, Nelson felt
for the safety of the Two Sicilies was largely due to the
influence of his adored mistress; that he was unwilling
to leave her, unwilling to expose her and her friends to
danger, and, not impossibly, convinced by her of the
vast importance of the kingdom to the allied cause.   It
must be remembered that his health was, throughout,
far from robust; that he was frequently ill, spending
days, apparently, on the couch, feverish, uneasy, hypo-
chondriacal; that the blow on the head a year before
had left him peevish, suspicious, irritable, opinionated.
But in addition to this, it must also be remembered that
this, though the most flagrant, was by no means the first
instance in which Nelson deliberately preferred his own
opinion or judgment to that of his commanding officer.
His disobedience at Naples in 1799 differed from that
at St. Kitts in 1785, or at Antigua in 1786, only in
degree; and his conduct in the battle of St. Vincent
might have been severely judged had any untoward

accident marred its effect. He decided rightly at Naples, as he did at St. Vincent, at Antigua, at St. Kitts, though the disobedience was more marked, the advantage more doubtful; but it would be fatal to the Navy and the country if it was once admitted that the opinion of a subordinate officer could be lightly put in comparison with the orders of the Commander-in-Chief.

Nelson's period of chief command was short and uneventful. The enemy had no naval force within the limits of the station, and the fleet was free to operate on the coast of Italy, reduce Capua and Gaeta, provide for the safety of Naples and Minorca, and keep up a strict blockade of Malta and Egypt. On August 1st the King dined on board the *Foudroyant*, and as he drank the victorious Admiral's health, all the Neapolitan ships and forts fired a royal salute of twenty-one guns. Nelson, describing the scene in a letter to his wife, wrote: "In the evening there was a general illumination. Amongst other representations, a large vessel was fitted out like a Roman galley; on its oars were fixed lamps, and in the centre was erected a rostral column with my name; at the stern were elevated two angels supporting my picture. The beauty of the whole is beyond my powers of description. More than 2000 variegated lamps were suspended round the vessel. An orchestra was fitted up, and filled with the very best musicians and singers. The piece of music was in a great measure to celebrate my praise, describing their previous distress, 'but Nelson came, the invincible Nelson, and they were preserved and again made happy.' This must not make you think me vain. No, very far from it; I relate it more from gratitude than vanity."

On August 5th, Nelson left Naples in the *Foudroyant*, carrying with him the King, who, within a few days after his return to Palermo, created him Duke of Bronte, and conferred on him the estate annexed to the title. This, Nelson understood, was worth about £3000 a year, but it does not appear that he ever received that much from it.   The letter officially informing him of the grant was dated August 13th, and in replying to this on the same day he first used the signature " Bronte Nelson," which, after receiving his own sovereign's sanction, he changed to " Nelson and Bronte."

In December Keith returned to the Mediterranean, writing to Nelson from off Oporto to put himself under his orders.   On arriving on the station, Keith went, in the first instance, to Mahon, where he had news of a French squadron fitting out for the relief of Malta.   At Leghorn he was met by Nelson with the further news of the Russians having withdrawn their ships from the blockade.   He resolved, therefore, to occupy the station which these had quitted, so as the better to intercept the French squadron if it should really come, which he thought scarcely probable.   Between Nelson and himself there seems to have been a difference of opinion as to placing the several ships ; and with a determination and carelessness of responsibility peculiar to him, Nelson, who was ordered to look out to the south-east, found himself, on the morning of February 18th, far to the north-west, and there, near the western extremity of Sicily, he fell in with the relieving force.   It consisted of the *Généreux* (which had escaped from the Nile and had afterwards captured the little *Leander*) with three corvettes and a large store-ship.   The corvettes scattered and made good their escape : the store - ship was taken possession of ; and the *Généreux*, by the gallant action of Captain Peard in the *Success* frigate, was stayed till the line-of-battle ships came up, when she struck her colours. Admiral Du Perrée, who commanded the squadron, was mortally wounded by a shot from the *Success*, and died on the following day. Keith naturally wrote that, "Lord Nelson has on this occasion, as on all others, conducted himself with skill and great address in comprehending my signals"; but Nelson more accurately wrote to his brother : "I have written to Lord Spencer, and sent him my journal to prove that the *Généreux* was taken by me and owing to my plan ; that my quitting Lord Keith was at my own risk, and for which, if I had not succeeded, I might have been broke."

On the 24th, Keith, who was anxious to get to Genoa (which, in co-operation with the Austrians, he afterwards reduced), directed Nelson to take command of the blockade of Malta. Nelson's reply in both a public and a private letter was to the effect that his health would not permit him to undertake the service, and that he should be obliged to go to his friends at Palermo. This has, of course, been attributed to his passion for Lady Hamilton, which would not permit him to be absent from her. There was, however, another reason which worked strongly in the same direction. He was excess-ively disgusted at having been superseded from the chief command, more especially by an officer newly appointed to the station ; and appears to have made up his mind from the first that he would not remain under Keith. It is not improbable that this feeling had at least something to do with his extraordinary refusal to

obey Keith's orders in the previous summer ; it is certain
that it was agitating his mind at this time. It appears
in all his letters ; in none perhaps more distinctly than
in one to Lord Minto of February 26th. "I have
serious thoughts," he wrote, " of giving up active service.
Greenwich Hospital seems a fit retreat for me after being
evidently thought unfit to command in the Mediterranean."

At any rate he was resolved not to stay off Malta ;
and though Troubridge and other friends wrote strongly,
imploring him not to quit the command, he could not be
prevailed on to continue. On March 10th he resigned
it to Troubridge, he himself returning to Palermo, where
he arrived on the 16th. He was, or perhaps rather
fancied himself, extremely ill. On March 20th he
wrote to Troubridge : "As yet it is too soon to form an
opinion whether I ever can be cured of my complaint.
. . . At present I see but glimmering hopes, and probably my career of service is at an end, unless the French
fleet shall come into the Mediterranean, when nothing
shall prevent my dying at my post. . . . *We of the Nile*
are not equal to Lord Keith in his estimation, and ought
to think it an honour to serve under such a clever man."

On the 24th, the *Foudroyant*, under the command of
Berry, was sent back to rejoin Troubridge, and had only
just come on the station when, on the night of the 29th,
the *Guillaume Tell*, blockaded in Valetta, made a gallant
attempt to escape. As she ran out of the harbour she
passed close by the *Penelope* frigate, commanded by
Captain Blackwood, who at all hazards followed her,
keeping up a continual fire to attract other ships.
Blackwood soon found that the *Penelope* was sailing
faster than the huge Frenchman, and remaining under

her stern, yawing now to port, now to starboard, poured
in an incessant raking fire, to which the *Guillaume Tell*,
not venturing to round to and demolish her puny
antagonist by a broadside, could make no effective reply.
Towards morning she had lost her main and mizen topmasts, and the 64-gun ship *Lion*, coming up, ranged
alongside and engaged her yard-arm to yard-arm, but
was quickly forced to drop astern. At six o'clock the
Foudroyant came up, and after a most gallant defence,
the *Guillaume Tell*, being totally dismasted, struck her
colours. She was crowded with men and had suffered
very great loss.

The news gave Nelson the most lively satisfaction.
She was the last of the Nile ships, and that she should
be captured by Berry commanding his flagship seemed a
fitting termination to his labours. On April 6th, he
wrote to Lord Minto : " Our dear, great Earl of St.
Vincent's orders to me were to follow the French Mediterranean fleet and to annihilate them. It has been
done, thanks to the zeal and bravery of my gallant
friends. My task is done, my health lost, and I have
wrote to Lord Keith for my retreat. May all orders be
as punctually obeyed, but never again an officer at the
close of what I must—without being thought vain—
call a glorious career, be so treated. I go with our dear
friends Sir William and Lady Hamilton ; but whether
by water or land depends on the will of Lord Keith."
All this and much more to the same effect seems to
prove that disgust at Lord Keith's appointment had
quite as much to do with his determination to go home
as his unwillingness to be separated from his mistress.

It was impossible for the Admiralty to tolerate this

thinly-veiled conduct, even in the victor of the Nile.
Any officer with less claim on the national gratitude
would have been summarily superseded. Lord Spencer
felt that Nelson deserved a certain allowance, and with
a delicate tact, at which even Nelson's sensitive nature
could not be offended, pointed out to him the disadvantage of the line he had taken. He could not, of course,
enter on the question of Keith's appointment as Commander-in-Chief, although he certainly knew the force of
that difficulty ; he dwelt rather on the impropriety and
inconvenience of his continued residence at Palermo. In
answer to Nelson's letter of March 20th, he wrote : "I
must express my extreme regret that your health should
be such as to oblige you to quit your station off Malta
at a time when I should suppose there must be the finest
prospect of its reduction. . . . If the enemy should
come into the Mediterranean . . . I should be much
concerned to hear that you learnt of their arrival in that
sea, either on shore or in a transport at Palermo." On
May 9th, the Admiralty sent out to Keith a formal permission for Nelson to return to England, if his health
rendered him incapable of doing his duty, and Lord
Spencer again wrote privately : "It is by no means my
wish or intention to call you away from service ; but
having observed that you have been under the necessity
of quitting your station off Malta on account of the state
of your health . . . it appeared to me much more advisable for you to come home at once than to be obliged
to remain inactive at Palermo while active service
was going on in other parts of the station. . . . I am
quite clear, and I believe I am joined in opinion by all
your friends here, that you will be more likely to recover

your health and strength in England than in an inactive
situation at a foreign court, however pleasing the respect
and gratitude shown to you for your services may be. . . .
I trust that you will take in good part what I have
taken the liberty to write to you as a friend."

It is unnecessary here to follow into the details of
this miserable scandal. It was perhaps better for the
service that it should be considered as altogether arising
out of feminine influence; and letters from old friends
in England as well as from Troubridge, a friend of his
boyhood, leave no doubt that the woman was generally
believed to be the cause of the evil. There can be no
question that she had a great deal to do with it,—a very
great deal; but the irritable jealousy not altogether
alien to Nelson's nature at the best of times, and at this
period aggravated by ill-health and the severe blow on
the head, must bear a large share of the blame.

Towards the end of April Nelson felt obliged to
return to Malta. The Hamiltons accompanied him in
the *Foudroyant*, a circumstance which not unnaturally
gave rise to many gross comments. The cruise lasted
through May, and on June 1st the *Foudroyant* again
arrived at Palermo. Nelson was extremely anxious to
take her to England. He had arranged that the
Hamiltons were to go with him. Keith, however, was
resolute. The destruction of the *Queen Charlotte*, a ship
of 100 guns, accidentally burnt off Leghorn on March
17th, was a serious loss to the fleet; and as no reinforcements were being sent from England, he deemed
it unadvisable to send a powerful ship, such as the
Foudroyant, off the station. He was perhaps also unwilling that the scandal, already in the air, should

appear to be sanctioned by the Commander-in-Chief. The *Seahorse*, he wrote to Nelson, would be at Mahon under orders for England. If he and his friends would go there, they might return in her or in any troopship they preferred, but he was quite unable to send either a line-of-battle ship or larger frigate.

Lady Hamilton had no particular wish to go by sea. She would have consented to take a passage in the *Foudroyant ;* she refused to do so in a trooper, and Nelson in this was entirely at her orders. They accordingly resolved to accompany the Queen to Vienna, and went, all together, to Leghorn in the *Foudroyant ;* thence to Ancona, where they took a passage to Trieste in a Russian frigate, with a Dalmatian captain and a Neapolitan first-lieutenant. The accommodation was cramped ; no preparations for distinguished visitors had been made ; the ship was in bad order, and Nelson was very ill. Hamilton too was seriously, it was feared dangerously, ill; and the voyage was wretched in the extreme.

At Vienna, where the party remained some days, Nelson was received with great distinction. On September 29th they were at Prague, where a grand *fête* in honour of his birthday was given by the Archduke Charles. Thence they went on to Dresden and stayed for a few days with Mr. Hugh Elliot, Lord Minto's brother, and at that time ambassador to the King of Saxony. There they met Mrs. St. George, a lively and imaginative young widow, who filled several pages of her letters and journal with exaggerated accounts of Nelson and his friends. That Lady Hamilton was exceedingly stout is perfectly true ; but notwithstanding her birth and want of education, she had been for twenty years intimately associated with men of refined manners and conversation, and must have acquired a certain veneer of politeness. Nelson, too, is always described, except by Mrs. St. George, as scrupulously moderate at table; and though he never had, nor aped, the manners of a fine gentleman, it appears certain that he had a natural and kindly courtesy which was very winning. At Dresden, indeed, he was in bad health and very much in love; and it may be that Mrs. St. George did not easily forgive his neglect of her for the sake of a fat, vulgar, immoral female.

CHAPTER VIII

THE BATTLE OF THE BALTIC

NELSON with his party, having taken ship at Hamburg, landed at Yarmouth on November 6th, and, as if to emphasise the cause of his leaving the Mediterranean, he at once wrote to the Admiralty to say that "his health being perfectly re-established, it was his wish to serve immediately." It was his home-coming after the battle of the Nile, and, as he stepped on shore, he was received by an enthusiastic crowd, the people taking the horses from the carriage and dragging it up to the hotel. The Mayor and Corporation waited on him with an address and the freedom of the town, which had been voted to him long before as a native of Norfolk. The next day he, always accompanied by Sir William and Lady Hamilton, and the Corporation attended a thanksgiving service in the church; and on leaving the town escorted by a bodyguard of cavalry, he left £50 with the Mayor for the poor.

One thing, however, was afterwards noticed, a thing indeed noticeable but, under the circumstances, not to be wondered at; Lady Nelson did not come to meet him. She was at the time with her father-in-law in London, staying at Nerot's Hotel in St. James's Street :

and there, on the evening of November 8th, Nelson
joined them. His reception by his wife is said to have
been extremely cold. It naturally was so. Already
she had judged his conduct and condemned him, on
popular rumour. There is no doubt whatever that, in
the ordinary phrase, she was an injured woman; but
it must in fairness be asked if some portion of the blame
did not rest with herself. Her husband had gained a
victory, the fame of which had resounded through
Europe; it is, perhaps, not too much to say that, during
the last months of 1798, his personal renown overtopped
that of any European warrior. He had won not only
glory but, compared with his former limited means,
fortune. He was wounded, he was ill; but Lady Nelson
contented herself with writing letters of extreme pro-
priety and remaining in England. Her partisans have
excused this; she was obliged, they say, to stay and
nurse her father-in-law, who was old and infirm. That
she did stay is certain; that there was any obligation
beyond her own choice is doubtful; the old man had
daughters and another daughter-in-law. The more
common opinion will be that, under the circumstances,
Lady Nelson's place was at her husband's side. To
leave him, whom she knew to be almost childishly vain
and sensitive, to the care of a kindly, beautiful and
fascinating courtesan, while she comforted him with
elegant epistles from a distance, surely deserves some of
the blame which our moral Pharisees have so freely
dealt out to her husband. As they now met with
feelings of disgust and irritation on both sides, it is
not to be wondered at that the breach was widened
by personal quarrels. There is no good reason to

doubt that "Emma" was the main cause of these.
"I am sick of hearing of 'Dear Lady Hamilton,'" Lady
Nelson is said to have exclaimed on one occasion ; probably enough she did so more than once.   But it is far
from improbable that the conduct of Lady Nelson's son
may have been angrily discussed ; that Lady Nelson
wished him to be recognised as her husband's sole heir ;
and that Nelson refused to have anything more to do
with him.

Of Josiah Nisbet very little is known, and that little
is not favourable.   He was at this time about twenty,
and by his stepfather's interest had been made lieutenant,
commander, and captain at an age when he ought to
have been still in the midshipmen's berth.   He seems
to have been of intemperate habits and boorish demean-
our.   When drunk, he was violent and insulting.   As
his father had died insane very shortly after his birth,
if not before it, it may be thought not impossible that
his vices were congenital.   Over and over again while
in the Mediterranean his misconduct had been pardoned
by St. Vincent or reproved by Nelson.   His mother was
naturally the one person who was blind to his faults ;
but if at this time she attempted to urge his interests
on her husband, it may well be that her representations
were received with peevish ill-humour or outbursts of
anger.   "Sooner than live the unhappy life I did when
last I came to England," Nelson wrote some three or
four months later, "I would stay abroad for ever."
Nothing is really known more than that they separated
by mutual agreement on January 13th, 1801, and did
not again see each other ; but Nelson, who was at all
times most generous in money matters, settled on her

£1200 a year, which, at the time, he could very ill afford.

Four days later he hoisted his flag on board the *San Josef* at Plymouth, with orders to join the fleet in Torbay under the command of Lord St. Vincent. This he did in the end of January; but St. Vincent was just at that time appointed First Lord of the Admiralty; and by the middle of February Nelson was directed to shift his flag to the *St. George* and put himself under the orders of Sir Hyde Parker, appointed Commander-in-Chief of the fleet going to the Baltic, or, as it was officially described, "on a particular service." On February 21st Nelson arrived at Spithead, on the 23rd he went to London on three days' leave; was back at Portsmouth on the 26th, and on March 2nd sailed with a squadron of seven ships of the line to join Sir Hyde at Yarmouth. The fleet sailed from Yarmouth on March 12th.

The two months prior to this date have a very curious interest in the story of Nelson's life. After more than two years of almost unbroken intercourse, he was forced to leave Lady Hamilton just as she was on the point of becoming a mother. On January 29th or 30th she gave birth to a female child, afterwards known as Horatia. The circumstances of the birth were carefully concealed, and the very fact was kept a close secret which has been fully revealed only within the last few years. But the discovery of Nelson's letters to Lady Hamilton written during these two months leaves no room for further doubt; for in these letters Nelson, addressing Lady Hamilton as "My own dear wife—for such you are in my eyes and in the face of

Heaven," repeatedly speaks of "our dear little child," the "dear pledge of love" which she had given him. "I firmly believe," he says in one, "that this campaign will give us peace, and then we will set off for Bronte, there to stay till your uncle dies," that is, Sir William Hamilton, and till he himself could be "separated from her," Lady Nelson.

Many of these letters are written as to Mrs. Thomson or Thompson (the name is spelt indifferently) on behalf of Mrs. Thomson's "dear friend," occasionally spoken of as Mr. Thomson ; and it has been suggested that Mr. Thomson was a real man, Mrs. Thomson a real woman, and that Nelson and Emma were merely go-betweens. A very slight examination of the correspondence shows that this is not so. The letters are all in Nelson's autograph, and whether written as from Nelson to Lady Hamilton or from Nelson to Mrs. Thomson in the name of her "dear friend," the sense is the same ; he will marry her as soon as her "uncle" dies and he is free. But beside this, the mistakes and confusion of persons in the Thomson letters are frequent. Here is one : " To Mrs. Thomson. Your good and dear friend does not think it proper at present to write with his own hand. . . . He swears before Heaven that he will marry you as soon as it is possible. . . . He charges me to say how dear you are to him. . . . I have given Lord N. £100 this morning, for which he will give Lady Hamilton an order on his agents, and I beg that you will distribute it amongst those who have been useful to you on the late occasion." It is almost unnecessary to add that there was no Thomson a friend of Nelson's, no Mrs. Thomson a friend of Lady Hamilton's.

The war now pending with the Baltic Powers, that is to say, with Russia, Sweden, and Denmark, arose out of what has been commonly called the Armed Neutrality, a treaty by which these northern Powers had bound themselves to resist the right of "visit and search" claimed by the belligerents, and to enforce the acceptance of certain principles of so-called international law : among others, the security of a belligerent's property under a neutral flag,—"a free ship makes free goods"; that a blockade to be binding must be maintained by an adequate force ; and that "contraband of war" must be distinctly defined beforehand. As these principles, if admitted by England, amounted to the import by France of naval stores,—masts, hemp, tar—from the Baltic, to be paid for by French exports, the English Government was resolved to contest them.

Such a confederation of the northern Powers had been attempted twenty years before, and had fallen to pieces by its own intrinsic weakness. The renewal of it in 1800 grew out of various incidents of the war, in which English frigates had enforced their right of visit and search of merchant-ships, even under convoy of a ship of war. These had been partially, and might have been wholly, arranged, when the news of the capture of Malta by the English upset the balance of the Russian Emperor's mind, and prompted him, possibly under the influence of French intrigue, to lay an embargo on English shipping in Russian ports, and to declare his determination to maintain the principles of the former armed neutrality. Sweden at once joined him, and Denmark was coerced, not perhaps unwillingly. Such a confederation, if allowed to mature itself under the presidency of an autocratic and irresponsible maniac, might evidently be a source of very great danger to England, and it was resolved to break it up,—by diplomacy, if possible, but if not, by force.

When the fleet sailed from Yarmouth, the Government would seem to have thought that Denmark would be easily detached from the confederation; and the instructions forwarded to Sir Hyde Parker,—instructions which must have been framed by Lord St. Vincent— were to proceed to Reval as soon as the fleet could be withdrawn from before Copenhagen; to attack the Russian squadron there; to destroy the arsenal; to pass on to Cronstadt; and, in general, "to attack and endeavour to capture or destroy any ships of war or others belonging to Russia, and to annoy that Power in every manner not incompatible with the fair and acknowledged usages of war."

These instructions were apparently discussed in a council of war on March 23rd; and on the 24th Nelson wrote a long letter to Sir Hyde, urging the necessity of prompt and immediate action if the negotiations at Copenhagen should prove unsuccessful, as, by the intelligence they had received from the ambassador, seemed now most probable. This letter is a full and masterly exposition of the prospects before them, and should be studied in detail by every one who wishes to obtain an insight into Nelson's manner of considering not merely how to get at the enemy, but, in his own words, "how to get at them with the least risk to our ships." It is impossible to do more here than indicate his definite proposals. "You are now," he wrote, "about Kronborg. If the wind be fair, and you deter-

mine to attack the ships and Crown Islands, you must
expect the natural issue of such a battle—ships crippled
and perhaps one or two lost; for the wind which carries
you in will most probably not bring out a crippled ship.
This mode I call taking the bull by the horns. It, however, will not prevent the Reval ships, or Swedes, from
joining the Danes; and to prevent this from taking
effect is, in my humble opinion, a measure absolutely
necessary—and still to attack Copenhagen. Two modes
are in my view : one to pass Kronborg, taking the risk
of damage, and to pass up the deepest and straightest
channel above the Middle Grounds; and coming down
the Garbar or King's Channel, to attack their floating
batteries, etc. etc., as we find it convenient. It must
have the effect of preventing a junction between the
Russians, Swedes, and Danes, and may give us an opportunity of bombarding Copenhagen. . . . Should this
mode of attack be ineligible, the passage of the Belt, I
have no doubt, would be accomplished in four or five
days, and then the attack by Dragör could be carried
into effect and the junction of the Russians prevented,
with every probability of success against the Danish
floating batteries. . . . Supposing us through the Belt
with the wind first westerly, would it not be possible to
either go with the fleet, or detach ten ships of three
or two decks, with one bomb or two fire-ships, to Reval,
to destroy the Russian squadron at that place ? I do
not see the great risk of such a detachment, and with
the remainder to attempt the business at Copenhagen.
The measure may be thought bold, but I am of opinion
the boldest measures are the safest."

It is of this last suggestion, "a suggestion worthy of

Napoleon himself," that Captain Mahan has well said :
"If adopted, it would have brought down the Baltic
Confederacy with a crash that would have resounded
throughout Europe." It was, however, the first pro-
posal which was ultimately adopted. When on the
30th the fleet passed Kronborg, entered the Sound, and
anchored a few miles to the north of Copenhagen, it was
seen, as Nelson had pointed out, that to go in from the
north, exposing the ships to the fire of the Crown
batteries, would be extremely dangerous, and could
scarcely lead to a satisfactory result. While off Elsinore, Nelson had shifted his flag to the *Elephant*, commanded by Captain Foley who had so brilliantly led into
action at the Nile, and he now at once volunteered to
undertake the attack in the way he had proposed, from
the southward, if the Admiral would give him ten ships
of the line and all the smaller vessels. Sir Hyde readily
agreed to this, giving him twelve ships of the line, and
leaving all the details to his judgment. In the *Amazon*
frigate he had already examined the position, and
during the night of March 31st had the channel by
which he was to pass carefully sounded. On the forenoon of April 1st the whole fleet moved on to an
anchorage within six miles of the town, off the north-
west end of the Middle Ground, a large shoal abreast of
Copenhagen, dividing the channel at that part into two.
By the easternmost of these the squadron under Nelson
passed the town out of range of the batteries ; and
having anchored for the night to the south-east of the
Middle Ground, examined the approach to the town
by the inner or King's Channel, and given detailed
orders to the several captains both in writing and

verbally, at half-past nine on April 2nd Nelson made the signal to weigh in succession.

The pilots, for the most part mates of small merchant vessels engaged in the Baltic trade, were unequal to the task of conducting these large ships in a channel from which the accustomed buoys had been removed, and Mr. Brierly, the master of the *Bellona*, piloted the squadron in, Captain George Murray leading in the *Edgar*. The second ship, the *Agamemnon*, keeping too much to the east, struck on the Middle Ground and remained fast; so also did the *Bellona* and *Russell;* the other nine ships passed up safely, and anchored abreast of the Danish floating batteries (heavily-armed hulks) ranged along the shoal water on the western side of the channel. At ten o'clock the action began. By half-past eleven the nine English ships had taken their positions, and the battle had become general. The two lines were about two hundred yards apart; the distance between the English ships was about one hundred. The *Elephant* was in the centre of the line, opposite to the Danish commodore, Fischer, in the *Dannebrog*.

At one o'clock the battle was raging fiercely. None of the Danish ships had been silenced; many of the English had suffered severely, and the *Bellona* and *Russell* had hoisted signals of distress. Seeing this, but unable to see what was actually taking place, Parker made the signal to discontinue the action. "Leave off action!" said Nelson; "damn me, if I do. You know, Foley, I have a right to be blind sometimes"; and putting the glass to his blind eye, continued, "I really do not see the signal." The story, told on the unimpeachable evidence of Colonel Stewart, who was by Nelson's side

at the time, and to whom part of the conversation was
addressed, has often been repeated as though marking
in a most characteristic way the man's reckless and
determined bravery. It is, however, very well established that Parker sent his flag-captain, Otway, with a
verbal message that the signal was to be understood as
permissive, and was made in that way so that the whole
responsibility might rest with Parker, if Nelson judged
it advisable to discontinue the action. If he thought it
advisable to continue it, he was at liberty to do so. He
judged it right to continue ; and the little pantomime
was only a joke, which Foley probably understood as
well as he did. Stewart apparently had no knowledge
of the message Otway had brought.

By two o'clock Nelson's resolution to continue the
action was clearly justified. Most of the Danish ships
had ceased to fire ; and as their crews were constantly
reinforced by men from the shore, the carnage on board
was very great. Some of them had their cables cut and
were drifting helplessly. The *Dannebrog* caught fire after
nearly every man on board had been killed or wounded,
and, drifting along the line, finally blew up, with the
loss of all that had been unable to jump overboard.
At half-past two, Nelson, seeing that this butchery (and
by this time it was nothing more) must go on as long as
the Danes continued sending fresh men to their ships,
wrote a letter to the Crown Prince, which was taken on
shore by Captain Sir Frederick Thesiger, serving on
Nelson's staff as a volunteer, who, having been in the
Swedish service, spoke the language sufficiently well.
This celebrated letter ran : "Lord Nelson has directions
to spare Denmark when no longer resisting ; but if the

firing is continued on the part of Denmark, Lord Nelson
will be obliged to set on fire all the floating batteries
he has taken, without having the power of saving the
brave Danes who have defended them. NELSON AND
BRONTE, Vice-Admiral, under the command of Admiral
Sir Hyde Parker. Dated on board his Britannic Majesty's
ship *Elephant*, Copenhagen Roads, April 2nd, 1801."
The letter brought on a truce, and the truce led to
an armistice which effectively detached Denmark from
the Confederation. It was suggested at the time, and
has since been often asserted, that the humanity which
appeared in the words of Nelson's letter was a mere
pretext, a subterfuge not altogether honourable, and
that the real motive of it was the hope of extricating
the squadron from a position of extreme danger ; for
that, even if the Danish hulks were completely silenced
or destroyed, the English squadron could not leave the
position they were in without becoming exposed to the
fire of the Three Crowns and other batteries, which they
were in no state to resist. There is no evidence in
support of such an allegation. Nelson himself most
positively denied its truth : the flag of truce, he asserted,
was sent for the sake of humanity, and for nothing else ;
and as a certain fact, patent to friends and enemies, he
made no attempt during the first hours of the truce to
get the ships out of the position they were in. A
message was sent to Parker, and till the answer came
and the truce was confirmed, it was uncertain whether
the action might not be renewed ; but during this time
none of the English ships even shifted berth ; where
they were at half-past two they still were at nightfall,
—when General Lindholm, who had been on board the

London, Parker's flagship, returned to Copenhagen, having agreed that hostilities were to be suspended for twenty-four hours and that the prizes were to be surrendered.

Nelson then returned to the *St. George* thoroughly worn out, having been awake all the previous night; though even then he could not go to bed without writing a few lines to Lady Hamilton. And these lines took the not very unusual form of verses, which Pettigrew, and others following him, have supposed to be Nelson's own composition. The most unlikely men, when sick of love, have been known to break into verse; but as these particular verses, sad rubbish though they are, are correct in their grammar and rhythm, but faulty in their seamanship, they cannot be Nelson's. The presumption is that they were Lord William Gordon's, who had constituted himself the poet of the lovers. "Recommend to Lord William not to make *songs* about us, for fear we should not deserve his good opinion," Nelson had written to Lady Hamilton only three days before; and these particular verses seemed to him an appropriate message of love as he hastily wrote them down and dated them : "*St. George*, April 2nd, 1801, at nine o'clock at night, very tired after a hard-fought battle."

Early on the following morning Nelson returned to the *Elephant*, still in the King's Channel, and was occupied during the day in refitting the ships and removing the prizes. The surrender of some of these was doubtful. The case of one has been a fertile source of legend and myth. According to Colonel Stewart's narrative, written at the time, a question arose whether the *Zealand* had struck or not, her pennant having been left flying.

Nelson went in person on board the Commodore's ship, which he found commanded by a Captain Müller whom he had known in the West Indies, and in friendly conversation with him succeeded in arranging the point in dispute. A similar difficulty about the surrender of the *Holstein*, which was overcome by a ruse of Captain Otway's, has been confused with this; and Nelson's meeting with Müller has been travestied in various ways into a meeting with a Lieutenant Willemoes whom he never saw.

On the 4th Nelson was instructed to visit the Crown Prince with power to negotiate an armistice, which, after some discussion, was concluded on the 9th. The term demanded by Nelson was fourteen weeks. To this the Danish Commissioners objected, urging their apprehension of the Court of Russia; on which Nelson, with most undiplomatic frankness, said that he wished to have time to act against the Russian fleet and return to Copenhagen. One of the Danes, in refusing to give way, spoke of a renewal of hostilities. Nelson knew sufficient French to understand what was said; and "Turning to one of his friends [probably Colonel Stewart, who relates the story], exclaimed with warmth, 'Renew hostilities! Tell him we are ready at a moment; ready to bombard this very night.'" The Commissioner apologised, but not till after long argument was the term insisted on by Nelson accepted.

The news of the victory reached London on the 15th, and on the 16th the two Houses of Parliament unanimously passed votes of thanks to Sir Hyde Parker, to Nelson, to Rear-Admiral Graves, to Colonel Stewart, and the officers, seamen, and marines of the fleet. And

in the House of Commons an address to the King was
agreed to, praying that a monument might be erected
in St. Paul's to the memory of Captain Mosse of the
Monarch, and of Captain Riou of the *Amazon*, who had
been killed in the battle.   No medal, however, was
given, and owing, it would seem, to some hint from the
Government, there was no complimentary vote from the
City of London ; two omissions which annoyed Nelson
exceedingly, and led him to write several vehement
letters both to Lord St. Vincent and to the Lord Mayor,
with whom, in consequence of the neglect, he point-
blank refused to dine.

On the 17th instructions were sent to Parker acquaint-
ing him with the death of the Emperor Paul on March
24th, and with the receipt of an amicable communication
from the Court of St. Petersburg.   The previous orders
for an attack on the Russian fleet at Reval were therefore suspended for the present.   He was directed to
ascertain the practical intentions of the Russian Government as soon as possible by sending a flag of truce ; and
to take action only if the overtures were absolutely
and positively rejected.   Four days later Parker was
recalled, and Nelson was appointed Commander-in-Chief.
Parker's delay both before the battle and afterwards,
his unwillingness to undertake anything on his own
responsibility, had convinced St. Vincent of the desira-
bility of having some one of a more energetic character
in command of the fleet, and he, at least, knew that
Nelson, with all his energy, was not the scatter-brained
fire-eater which some people had supposed him.

The change took effect on May 5th, and Nelson, who
had already vainly urged on Parker the advisability of

taking the fleet to the Gulf of Finland, immediately
made the signal to prepare for sea. He was firmly convinced that the negotiations would be more satisfactory
if the Russian Government realised the danger of delay ;
and was anxious at any rate to prevent the two Russian
squadrons from joining, or the Russians "mixing the
affairs of Denmark or Sweden with the detention of
English ships."

On the 7th the fleet sailed from Kiöge Bay, where
it had lain ever since the conclusion of the armistice ;
and, leaving Captain Murray as senior officer with seven
sail of the line and all the bombs, fire-ships, etc., at Born-
holm, Nelson with eleven ships of the line, a frigate
and two sloops, came, on May 12th, off Reval, where,
much to his disappointment, he found that the Russian
squadron had got through the ice and gone to Cronstadt
only a few days before. In his letters he repeatedly
asserts that the English fleet might and ought to have
been there on April 2nd, when the squadron would
have been entirely at their mercy. "Nothing," he
wrote, "if it had been right to make the attack, could
have saved one ship of them in two hours after our
entering the bay." It may be added that, if Parker
could have considered the strategy of the campaign with
the genius of his subordinate, the useless slaughter and
maiming of nine hundred and forty-three Englishmen
and double that number of Danes would have been
avoided ; for the Czar had been put to death on March
24th, and his son Alexander had no wish to continue the
hostile policy of his father.

None the less, the Russian Government was unwilling
now to appear to yield to pressure ; and on May 16th

Nelson received a letter from the Russian Secretary, Count Pahlen, stating the Emperor's surprise at the appearance of such a force in Russian waters while the English Government was professing peaceful intentions, and imperatively requiring him to remove it. "I do not believe he would have written such a letter if the Russian fleet had been in Reval," was Nelson's comment on it to Lord St. Vincent. He, however, at once sailed out of the Gulf, and being in very feeble health, begged St. Vincent to relieve him from the command. "Since the 27th of April," he wrote on May 17th, "I have not been out of my cabin, except in being obliged to do the civil thing at Reval; nor do I expect to go out until I land in England, or am carried out of the ship." It was, too, just at this time that he received news of the death of his brother Maurice, a clerk in the Navy Office. "It has naturally affected me a good deal," he wrote; "if I do not get some repose very soon, another will go. Six sons are gone out of eight." That his health at this time was not good, we know on the authority of Colonel Stewart, who wrote: "His mind was not at ease; with him, mind and health invariably sympathised."

Nevertheless his statements should perhaps not be taken quite literally. Colonel Stewart's account of his mode of life does not represent him as a man at the point of death or anywhere near it. After speaking of the attention he paid to the health of his fleet and the economical expenditure of stores, Stewart continued: "His hour of rising was four or five o'clock, and of going to rest about ten; breakfast was never later than six, and generally nearer to five o'clock. A midshipman or two were always of the party; and I have known him

send during the middle watch to invite the little fellows
to breakfast with him when relieved. At table with
them, he would enter into their boyish jokes, and be the
most youthful of the party. At dinner he invariably
had every officer of the ship in their turn, and was both
a polite and hospitable host. The whole ordinary
business of the fleet was invariably despatched, as it had
been by Earl St. Vincent, before eight o'clock. The
great command of time which Lord Nelson thus gave
himself, and the alertness which this example imparted
throughout the fleet, can only be understood by those
who witnessed it, or who know the value of early hours."

After a week or ten days in Rostock Bay, by the
beginning of June he was again in Kiöge Bay. On the
13th he received permission to return to England, and
at the same time instructions to invest Rear-Admiral
Graves with the order of the Bath, which was done with
much ceremony on the quarter-deck of the *St. George*
on June 14th, Nelson laying the sword on the Rear-
Admiral's shoulder in the name of the King. A few
days later Sir Charles Pole arrived to relieve him, and
on the 19th Nelson sailed for England in the *Kite* brig,
leaving a farewell address to the admirals, captains,
officers, and men, thanking them for the noble and honourable support they had given him, and attributing the
extraordinary good health of the fleet "to the regularity,
exact discipline, and cheerful obedience of every individual in it"; but, as if to mark that his praise was not
a mere complimentary form, he specially excepted the
officers of two of the gun-brigs and a bomb.

Nelson landed at Yarmouth on July 1st, and after
visiting the hospitals to which the wounded at Copen-

hagen had been sent, went on to London. He had
already, by patent of May 22nd, been raised to the
dignity of a viscount under the title of Viscount Nelson
of the Nile and Burnham Thorpe ; and was now consulted as to his wish that, in default of his issue male,
the barony might be continued to his father's heirs-
male, or failing them, to the heirs-male of his sisters,
Mrs. Bolton and Mrs. Matcham respectively ; and this
was finally prescribed by the patent of August 18th.

Meantime he was requested both by Mr. Addington
and Lord St. Vincent to take command of a very considerable force of frigates, brigs, and smaller vessels for
the defence of the coast between Orfordness and Beachy
Head, against some part of which it was understood the
French were preparing an attack. It was a particular
service, independent of the command in the Downs, then
held by Nelson's old captain, now Admiral Lutwidge ;
but St. Vincent quite well understood the delicacy of
the situation, and that the appointment of a junior to an
independent command in the Narrow Seas could not but
be, in some respects, unpleasant to the older officer. St.
Vincent's explanations, however, seem to have been taken
in good part ; and by the real wish on all sides to act for
the good of the public service, and by forbearance and
tact on one side and the other, there seems to have been
absolutely no friction.

On preparing to assume his command, Nelson submitted to the Admiralty a paper stating his views on the
defence of the river. He conceived that the object of
the French would be London, and that for that they
must aim at getting on shore as speedily as possible ;
"the dangers of a navigation of forty-eight hours"

appeared to him "an insurmountable objection to the rowing from Boulogne to the coast of Essex." Hence he judged that from Boulogne, Calais, or even Havre, they would try and land on the south coast of Kent or Sussex; or from Dunkirk, Ostend, and other parts of Flanders, on the coast of Essex or Suffolk; and he pointed out the necessity of ascertaining the number of small vessels in each port. He thought they might mean to attempt to surprise London with forty thousand men, and for that, to land twenty thousand west of Dover and twenty thousand north of the Thames. For this from two hundred to two hundred and fifty boats must be collected at Boulogne and the neighbouring ports, and as many at Dunkirk and the ports of Flanders; and on this supposition he elaborated his plan of defence. Two days later, on July 27th, he hoisted his flag on board the *Unité* frigate at Sheerness, but after a few days shifted it to the *Medusa*.

As soon as he could examine the situation for himself, he began to realise that the alarm which had been felt was quite unfounded. On August 2nd he wrote that fifty or sixty was the full number of boats, large and small, at Boulogne; on the 3rd, that "of the craft which I have seen, I do not think it possible to row them to England, and sail they cannot." On the 4th he had over some bombs, which presently sank some five of the enemy's largest vessels. "I think I may venture to assure you," he wrote to Addington, "that the French army will not embark at Boulogne for the invasion of England"; and on the 6th he wrote to Lord St. Vincent: "The information respecting the number of troops assembled at Boulogne cannot be true; it is evidently a lie, most likely fabricated by some scoundrel emigrant in London. I have now more than ever reason to believe that the ports of Flushing and Flanders are much more likely places to embark men from than Calais, Boulogne or Dieppe; for in Flanders we cannot tell by our eyes what means they have collected for carrying an army." On the 7th he wrote again : " I pronounce that no embarkation can take place at Boulogne; whenever it comes forth, it will be from Flanders; and what a forlorn undertaking! Consider cross tides, etc. etc. As for rowing, that is impossible. It is perfectly right to be prepared against a mad government; but with the active force your lordship has given me, I may pronounce it impracticable."

He was less successful in obtaining some intelligence of the state of the enemy's preparations in the ports of the Low Countries, and could only hope they might make the attempt for which he was fully prepared. " In my command," he wrote from Margate on August 12th, "I find much zeal and good-humour, and should Mr. Bonaparte put himself in our way, I believe he will wish himself even in Corsica. I only hope, if he means to come, that it will be before September 14th, for my stamina is but ill suited for equinoctial gales and cold weather." The next day, however, he had more definite information. " The account of troops given by the French scoundrels in our pay is as false as they are. I am certain that in the towns of Boulogne and the surrounding hills the total number could not exceed two thousand men. The *Galgo* arrived in the night from off Ostend. Captain Hawkins assures me that the boats collected at Ostend and Blankenberg may amount to sixty or seventy;

that he is sure they could not carry more than fifty or sixty men each; he understood that the poor devils of fishermen are sent off for Brest. Where, my dear lord, is our invasion to come from?"

It is well thus to trace the growth of Nelson's conviction, and to see how, starting with the belief that the attempt was one likely to be made in serious earnest, he became convinced, after a fortnight's careful study of the problem, that success was so utterly impossible that it was practically certain the attempt would not be made. Having arrived at this conclusion, he wished to assume the offensive and to punish the enemy for the insolent pretence which they had put forth. His plan was carefully drawn up; four divisions of boats, amounting in the aggregate to fifty-seven, were to row silently and by night into the harbour of Boulogne, and bring out or set fire to all the enemy's boats therein.

The attempt was made on the night of August 15th-16th; but though the flotilla moored in the mouth of the harbour was reached, it was found that the vessels were fastened to the shore and to each other with chains which could not be cut, nor in the darkness unshackled. Many of them were boarded and carried; but such a heavy fire of musketry was opened on them from the shore, that they could not be held even long enough to set them on fire. The attacking force was obliged to retreat not only without success, but having sustained a severe loss in killed and wounded.

Nelson's letters on this occasion would of themselves go far to explain the enthusiastic affection with which he was regarded by those under his command. His force had suffered a disastrous repulse; he might well expect his conduct to be harshly criticised, and the defeat must have been a cruel blow to his vanity. But his vanity, though prominent in success, seems to have been altogether absent in the hour of misfortune. He did not, as smaller men might have done, attempt to defend himself by showing that the fault did not lie with him; that his instructions had been departed from, his orders disobeyed, the assault weakly conducted. On the contrary, he declared: "The most astonishing bravery was evinced by many of our officers and men. . . . No person can be blamed for sending them to the attack but myself. . . . All behaved well : it was their misfortune to be sent on a service which the precautions of the enemy rendered impossible to succeed in"; and many more sentences of the same kind he wrote to the Admiralty, to Lord St. Vincent, and to Mr. Addington.

Notwithstanding the defeat of August 16th, Nelson was by no means satisfied of the impossibility of getting at the French boats, and several of his letters at this time contain suggestions or proposals of an attack on them at Flushing, or wherever they were. On October 3rd he proposed to St. Vincent " to run a fire-brig into Boulogne harbour the first fresh northerly wind "; or, failing that, "to make an 'infernal' of one of the bombs, and to have fire-boats, etc., to keep them for ever in hot water." "However," he added, "if we are on the eve of peace, it would be a bad reconciliation "; and in fact the very next day, October 4th, he had news of the preliminaries being signed.

A week later the French ambassador arrived in London with the ratification of the preliminaries, and was received by the people with enthusiastic delight. " Can

you cure madness?" Nelson wrote to Dr. Baird, "for I am
mad that our damned scoundrels dragged a Frenchman's
carriage. I am ashamed for my country." Nelson, in
fact, had no love for the French, either in peace or war,
and as he had written to Louis at Gaeta in 1799, " There
is no way of dealing with a Frenchman but to knock
him down," so now; and again in 1803 he wrote : "I
would not upon any consideration have a Frenchman
in the fleet, except as a prisoner. Forgive me ; but my
mother hated the French." Of his mother's likes or
dislikes, Nelson could not possibly know much ; but
when we are inclined to think his frequent expressions
of hatred and distrust unworthy of a great mind, we
ought to remember that for the last ten years Nelson
had seen nothing but the seamy side of the French
character, and that to him the names of Frenchman and
low-bred ruffian were practically synonymous. Nor was
he at all singular in his dislike : it was a feature of the
age ; and, as is well known, Nelson's royal friend the
Duke of Clarence could scarcely bring himself to be
civil to his French guests, even when King, thirty or
five-and-thirty years later.

However, now that the preliminaries were ratified,
Nelson was anxious to be relieved from his command,
and grumbled bitterly because the Admiralty thought it
right not to relieve him immediately. With Troubridge
he was more especially angry. Troubridge was his old
friend and messmate : Troubridge, he thought, owed
him something for insisting on the recognition of his
services in the Mediterranean, and getting him the
baronetcy ; but now Troubridge seemed the principal
hindrance to his going on shore. Of the many letters

which he wrote to Lady Hamilton about this time, there
is scarcely one which does not contain some petulant
expressions regarding him. " I daresay," he wrote on
October 20th, " Master Troubridge is grown fat.   I
know I am grown lean with my complaint, which, but
for their indifference about my health, would never have
happened ; or at least I should have got well long
ago in a warm room, with a good fire and sincere
friends."

It is, of course, an old-established belief among
naval officers that the Admiralty, having neither body
nor soul, has no fear of punishment in either this world
or the next ; but we may reasonably suppose that
Nelson's valued and tried friends St. Vincent and
Troubridge did not keep him afloat merely to sport
with his ill-health, but rather because they judged it
safer not to disarm in too great a hurry ; and probably
they understood that Nelson's chief complaint was a discontented longing to be with his mistress. Troubridge, at
least, was familiarly acquainted with the truth and the
scandal of Nelson's life at Palermo ; and though neither
he nor his chief wished to pose as a censor of morals,
neither of them considered the love-sick Admiral's
" pleasant vices " a sufficient excuse for modifying the
requirements of the service.

CHAPTER IX

AT length, however, Nelson obtained leave of absence. On October 22nd he struck his flag and hurried to Merton, a place in Surrey, some eight or nine miles from Piccadilly, which he had commissioned Lady Hamilton to buy for him. Much of his correspondence during the previous month refers directly or indirectly to this and his wishes respecting it. The purchase was completed about the end of September or beginning of October, Davison writing that Nelson was to draw on him for any money he might want. Lady Hamilton was a good woman of business when her insatiable vanity or restless love of pleasure did not interfere; and she seems to have concluded this transaction with quickness, economy, and good taste. "You will do what is right," Nelson wrote to her, "and I should be happy in leaving everything to your management. I trust to your economy, for I have need of it; but I do earnestly request that all may be mine in the house, even to a pair of sheets, towels, etc."

On October 16th Sir William Hamilton wrote to Nelson: "We have now inhabited your Lordship's premises some days, and I can now speak with some certainty. I have lived with our dear Emma several years ; I know her merit, have a great opinion of the head and heart that God Almighty has been pleased to give her ; but a seaman alone could have given a fine woman full power to choose and fit up a residence for him without seeing it himself. You are in luck, for on my conscience, I verily believe that a place so suitable to your views could not have been found, and at so cheap a rate ; for if you stay away three days longer, I do not think you can have any wish but you will find it completed here. And then, the bargain was fortunately struck three days before an idea of peace got abroad. Now every estate in the neighbourhood has increased in value, and you might get a thousand pounds to-morrow for your bargain."

This was the place to which Nelson now retired, and at which or at Hamilton's house, No. 23 Piccadilly, with but few breaks he spent the next fifteen or sixteen months ; the Hamiltons and he living together and sharing the household expenses, which were very large, for Lady Hamilton, though no longer a young woman, had an insatiable craving for gaiety, and the house was seldom without visitors. The weekly payments varied very much, from under £30 to over £100 ; but taken one with another, they seem to have averaged about £60, or £3000 a year. The lowest amount is £27 ; but immediately following it is £77, and for one week it is as much as £218 ; of which, however, £103 is to the wine-merchant, and £9 : 19 : 6 for maraschino ; which would seem to imply that Lady Hamilton was in both respects ready to do justice to the alliterative toast proposed as the feminine equivalent of the masculine "Wine and Women."

N

Hamilton had formerly been fond of society; but he was now feeling the full weight of his seventy-one years and of the free living in which he had indulged through the greater part of them.   He wanted rest; he wanted to make his own arrangements; he objected to having twelve or fourteen at table every day, and those constantly changing.   He was discontented and out of his discontent came friction.   So, turning the matter over in his mind, he put his thoughts on paper in an extraordinary memorandum to his wife, in which, stating his several grievances, he resolved that a separation would be preferable to a continuance of "silly altercations"; but as he was not likely to trouble "any party" much longer, it would be best for them to "bear and forbear"; more especially as a separation would make Lord Nelson, "our best friend, very uncomfortable," and "would be more sensibly felt by him than by us."   "I well know," he added, "the purity of Lord Nelson's friendship for Emma and me."

On April 26th, 1802, Nelson's father died at Bath. He was then in his seventy-ninth year and had been failing for some time.   His relations with his son had been always affectionate; but as Lady Nelson was much with the old man, her husband had seen little or nothing of him since his return from the Baltic.   He certainly did not attend the funeral, being at the time at Merton. In July and August he, with the Hamiltons, made a tour into Wales.   As they passed through Oxford he received an honorary degree, and on visiting Monmouth, Hereford, and Worcester, was admitted to the freedom of those cities.   By the beginning of September he was back at Merton, and there he remained till the end of the year.

The party then moved to Piccadilly, and there on April 6th, 1803, Sir William Hamilton died. He had been failing for some months, and during his last illness was affectionately attended by both his wife and Nelson. It is difficult to conceive anything more strange than the relations of the three at this time. Nelson and Hamilton were on terms of the closest friendship, each one expressing the warmest affection and esteem for the other. For the last six nights of Hamilton's life, Nelson sat by his bedside ; and at his death, Nelson held his hand while his wife supported his pillow. A few hours later Nelson wrote to the Duke of Clarence : " My dear friend Sir William Hamilton died this morning ; the world never, never lost a more upright and accomplished gentleman." To Davison he wrote on the same day : " Poor Lady Hamilton is, as you may expect, desolate." And yet we know now, by the evidence of letters in Nelson's own writing, that for at least three years he had been dishonouring this dear friend, that he was the father of " poor Lady Hamilton's " little girl, and that the two had been calculating on, if not wishing for, the " upright and accomplished gentleman's " death.

Was this all hypocrisy ? In most cases the answer would be an unhesitating " Yes " ; in this particular case it may be a doubting " No." There is at least room to believe that Nelson had persuaded himself, or had been persuaded by his mistress, that she was Hamilton's wife only in name ; that he had married her only to have a lady at the head of his table. His most intimate letters to Emma always refer to Sir William as her " uncle," and he addressed her as the " most virtuous of women," which, if he had known or suspected her antecedents, would surely have been most bitter irony. But the position is a psychological puzzle which does not admit of any quite satisfactory solution.

Meantime the prospect of a renewal of hostilities had been occupying Nelson's thoughts, and before the end of March it was settled that, in such an event, he should go to the Mediterranean as Commander-in-Chief. After some weeks of uncertainty war was declared on May 16th, and with a prompt despatch which the English Government has not always shown, Nelson's commission was dated on the very same day; on the 18th he hoisted his flag on board the *Victory* at Portsmouth, and put to sea on the 20th. His specific instructions were to proceed off Toulon with such part of the squadron under his command as he might judge adequate to the service, and take such a position as he should consider most proper for enabling him to take, sink, burn, or otherwise destroy any ships or vessels belonging to France or French citizens; to detain any Dutch ships which he might fall in with; to keep watch on the conduct of the Court of Spain, as well as of any naval preparations that might be made in Spanish ports; and to prevent any squadron of Spanish ships of war from entering a French port or forming a junction with a French or Dutch squadron.

On May 17th Admiral Cornwallis had sailed from Plymouth to institute a close blockade of Brest; on the 19th he was off the port; and as it was judged advisable to strengthen his fleet as much as possible against any immediate attempt at evasion, Nelson was directed to communicate with him in passing, and if he wished it, to leave the *Victory* with him and proceed to the Mediter-

ranean in the *Amphion* frigate. Off Ushant, however,
he did not succeed in meeting Cornwallis; and as it
seemed necessary for him to get to Toulon without
delay, he left the *Victory* with orders to follow him as
soon as Cornwallis could spare her, and pursued his
voyage in the *Amphion*.

After touching at Malta on June 15th and passing
Naples on the 25th, on July 8th he joined the fleet off
Toulon.   The force at his disposal was curiously small,
considering the numerous and varied duties which he
was called on to perform.   Nine French ships of the
line, with five frigates, were said to be in Toulon.   Seven
ships of the line were clearly to be seen.   The squadron
with Nelson at this time consisted of nine ships of the
line, two of which were of 64 guns; all were foul from
having been long from England, were weakly manned
and sickly.   With these Nelson undertook the military
blockade of the port, and carried it through with a
stringency that has never been paralleled.   Brest was,
indeed, repeatedly blockaded during the war, but with
larger force and continual reinforcements or refreshments from Plymouth.   Off Toulon Nelson's squadron
was generally inferior in point of numbers to the enemy,
and with the absolutely small size of the squadron the
inferiority was large in proportion.   Reinforcements
seldom reached him; refreshments there were none,
except what he himself ordered; he had no dockyard,
no stores, no base to fall back on; everything had to be
provided for by himself.   It was in this more than in
the prolonged duration of the effort that the exceptional
nature of the blockade consisted.

In giving some account of this remarkable service, it

is well to explain that, while a commercial blockade consists in absolutely sealing the port, so that no merchant-ship can attempt to enter or leave it without incurring the most serious risk of being captured and the certainty of being condemned, a military blockade is merely watching the port with a force sufficient to bring the enemy's squadron to action should it come out. To keep up such a watch effectively requires a numerical strength which can spare a few ships and remain adequate for the service; but this strength Nelson never had. While the French were continually adding to the force of their squadron within, so that they raised their numbers from seven to eleven or even twelve ships of the line, Nelson seldom had off Toulon more than eight or nine, in consequence of the requirements of other parts of the station. He was thus generally unable to send the ships away for rest and refreshment by ones or twos at a time: the provisions were brought to the fleet where it was; and when the water began to run short, the whole fleet went to Maddalena, where the magnificent anchorage had been discovered and surveyed by Captain Ryves of the *Agincourt*, in whose honour Nelson named it Agincourt Sound. Of late years the Italians have followed Nelson's lead, and have made it a fortified roadstead.

The attempt to trace the story of the blockade from day to day would be as tedious in the reading as the blockade itself was in the execution; it will be sufficient to indicate Nelson's method, and to notice the occasional breaks in the terrible monotony, which of itself was exceedingly apt to wear out both officers and men. When Nelson joined the fleet, there was a good deal of scurvy ; onions and lemons would, he thought, eradicate it, or "a sight of the French squadron twenty leagues at sea would cure all complaints." The onions and lemons, however, had to do the work alone ; and in summer or in winter, in fine weather or in foul, this squadron maintained a watch off Toulon for upwards of eighteen months without a break, save an occasional visit to Agincourt Sound ; and at the end of the time the men were not only in better health than at the beginning, but were in absolutely good health.

Those writers who have described Nelson as a mere fighting hero have falsified both his character and his history. He was not more pre-eminent in the day of battle than he was in his attention to the thousand details which kept his men in good health, his ships in good order, and his fleet invincible. It has even been said, by some who mistake the means for the end, that his discipline was slack and his ships never in good order. There is an old proverb which says, "The proof of the pudding is in the eating"; and the best test of good discipline and good order is the ability to fight and to crush a superior enemy, a test which has no relation to the harassing of the men with ceaseless drill, or wearing them out with unmeaning work, and all the "spit and polish" which towards the close of the war came to be thought the thing most to be desired, till, amid misfortune and disaster, Broke brought the service back to understand that there really were things of more importance. And so it was with Nelson. The men were not wearied and disgusted with useless labour or needless restrictions ; the constant exercise at sea, often in tempestuous weather, gave them sufficient occupation, while every possible care was taken of their health and comfort.

By the report of the physician to the fleet in August 1805, it was shown that out of a force varying between six and eight thousand men, the total number of deaths during two years of exceptionally hard service was one hundred and ten, and the average number of men on the sick-list was one hundred and ninety, or twenty-five per thousand; whereas it appeared by a report of Sir Gilbert Blane's that in 1781, out of a force of twelve thousand men, fifteen hundred and seventy-seven had died in one year; of which number only fifty-nine had been killed or died of wounds; and that the average number on the sick-list was one in fifteen, or sixty-seven per thousand. Hawke and St. Vincent had already shown that it was possible to keep a fleet effective during a long period of arduous service; but it was for Nelson to show that the period of arduous service might be one of exceptionally good health with the death-rate reduced to a minimum.

The causes of this extraordinary result were: the attention paid to the victualling and purveying for the fleet; the issue of good wholesome wine instead of spirits; of fresh beef as often as it could possibly be procured; vegetables and fruit whenever they could be purchased; and an abundant supply of excellent sweet water allowed to the ships' companies. The ships were kept dry and well ventilated; there was no idleness intemperance, skulking, or malingering, for there were no spirits and there was no hospital. The sick were comfortably accommodated, placed on regular sick-diet, and supplied with fresh meat, vegetables, fruit, soft bread, etc. Peruvian bark in wine or spirits was regularly served out to the men employed in wooding or watering; and cheerfulness among the men was promoted and encouraged by music, dancing, and theatrical amusements, the example of which was given by the Commander-in-Chief in the *Victory*. All these may seem mere prosaic details; but life is made up of details, as an hour is made up of seconds. It was the unceasing care and attention to these details that kept the men healthy, that rendered the long blockade possible, and that ensured a victory when, after long waiting, the enemy was at last met.

On July 30th the *Victory* joined the fleet, and Nelson at once hoisted his flag on board her, Hardy accompanying him as flag-captain, and George Murray, who had commanded the *Edgar* at Copenhagen, being with him as Captain of the Fleet. The Captain of the Fleet, who is either a rear-admiral or has temporary rank as such, is the chief of the staff of the Commander-in-Chief, and is mainly responsible to him for the due performance of all routine; he is supposed to keep him fully informed on all points of detail, and to consult with him as to the several requirements of the different ships; but not to originate plans or to issue orders, except in subordination to the Admiral. Attempts have, of course, frequently been made to assign to the Captain of the Fleet the credit of all that emanates from the Commander-in-Chief, as in the celebrated discussion that was raised about Rodney's great victory over De Grasse; but it is quite certain that Nelson owed nothing to Murray, except that good and zealous co-operation which, indeed, he got from every officer who came under his command.

Nelson's letters, memorandums, and orders during the whole time show that not only in name but in reality he directed and provided for everything.

From the first he believed that the French meant to come out as soon as they fancied themselves strong enough. Of their aim he could only guess; but in view of what they afterwards actually did, his speculations concerning it are extremely interesting. He took for granted that they intended to invade Sardinia; but that, he thought, would be done by a military expedition fitted out from Marseilles. It is, however, specially notable that as early as August 25th, 1803, he wrote to Mr. Addington: "My station to the westward of Toulon, an unusual one, has been taken upon an idea that the French fleet is bound out of the Straits, and probably to Ireland. It is said ten thousand men are collecting at Toulon. I shall follow them to the Antipodes." And the next day he wrote to Sir Richard Strachan, then senior officer at Gibraltar: "I wish to call your serious attention to what I am going to mention. The French fleet being perfectly ready for sea, seven of the line, six frigates, and some corvettes—two sail of the line are now rigging in the arsenal—I think it more than probable that they are bound to the westward, out of the Mediterranean. Therefore, as I am determined to follow them, go where they may, I wish you, in case they escape me, to send a frigate or sloop after them to find out their route, giving her a station where I may find her; and keep yourself either at the mouth of the Straits or off Europa Point, for I certainly shall not anchor at Gibraltar."

It does not appear that he ever considered the contemplated evasion to be connected with a plan for the

invasion of England, and we may believe that he would
have pronounced such a scheme altogether outside the
possibilities of naval war; but we see that from the first
he suspected their intention of going out of the Mediterranean, and made up his mind to follow them; whatever their aim, he was determined to be one of the party.
This determination, from which he never wavered, seems
to explain his manner of watching the port. He wished
to fight the French as soon as they should be clear of
the harbour; but over and over again he expressed his
resolve not to hazard his ships against their batteries,
nor even against their fleet till he had it in such a position that they could not slip back into Toulon after an
indecisive action, leaving the English fleet crippled and
obliged to raise the blockade.

This care for his ships, this resolve to do nothing
rashly, is repeatedly expressed in language which was
none the less stringent for being couched in friendly or
even in affectionate terms. Writing, for instance, to
Strachan and explaining his views as to the probability
of war with Spain and the possibility of the Spaniards
protecting the *Aigle*, a French 74 which Strachan was
blockading in Cadiz, he concluded thus: "Recollect that
it would be much better to let the French ship escape
than to run too great a risk of losing the *Donegal*, yourself, and ship's company." A still more marked instance
of this care and this resolve appears in a letter of May
24th, 1804. On that day Rear-Admiral Campbell in the
Canopus of 80 guns, with the *Donegal* of 74 and the
Amazon frigate, was close in with Cape Sepet, while the
main body of the fleet was out of sight to seaward. Five
French ships of the line, with three frigates and several

gunboats, came out of the harbour, in the evident
intention of cutting off the small reconnoitring squadron.
Campbell of course made sail away from them, and the
French, unwilling to risk even the possibility of being
drawn too far from the shelter of their port, gave up the
pursuit. It was not till six hours later that the *Canopus*
and her consorts rejoined the fleet. It was then that
Nelson wrote to the Rear-Admiral : " I am more obliged
to you than I can express for your not allowing the very
superior force of the enemy to bring you to action.
Whatever credit would have accrued to your own and
your gallant companions' exertions, no sound advantages
could have arisen to our country, for, so close to their
own harbour, they could always have returned, and left
your ships unfit, probably, to keep the sea. I again, my
dear Admiral, thank you for your conduct."

Many more instances might be quoted, all tending to
the same point, to show how, with all his resolution to
fight, he was no hot-brained bully to run needless or
useless risks, still less to have his ships beaten to pieces
against stone walls and solid fortifications. When in
1854 the country howled against Sir Charles Napier
because in the course of a few summer months he did
not take or destroy the massive fortifications of Cronstadt
and the enemy's fleet behind them, it would have been
well had it been reminded that neither Hawke nor
Nelson, St. Vincent nor Cornwallis, had cared to lay
their ships against the far inferior defences of Toulon,
of Brest, or even of Cadiz ; that so long as the enemy's
fleet remained within these defences it was practically
safe. When it came out, Hawke had for all time laid
down a lesson as to what to do with it.

Through the summer of 1804 it was the custom of
the French Admiral, M. La Touche-Tréville (the *ci-devant*
Comte de la Touche-Tréville), every now and then to
get a few ships under way in the outer roadstead, and
when the wind favoured him, to come out a short
distance, and return. It was a very proper exercise,
and the only way in which he could give his men some
little sea-training. It happened that at different periods
of his career Nelson had been unfavourably impressed
by La Touche-Tréville's conduct. It was he who in
1780, in command of the 36-gun frigate *Hermione*, sailed
from Boston after arrogantly pledging himself to clear
the coast of British frigates, and a few days later was
defeated and put to flight by the 32-gun frigate *Iris*.
It was he who, in December, 1792, had been sent to
Naples to enforce the demands of the Republic, and had
executed his mission with an insolence which, we may
be sure, was not softened in the narration which reached
Nelson's ears. And again, it was he who had commanded at Boulogne in August, 1801, and whose precautions had convicted Nelson of an error. It can
scarcely be doubted that this was, in Nelson's eyes, an
aggravation of what the English, at any rate, called his
poltroonery at Boston and his insolence at Naples. In
reality he seems to have been a capable officer, as officers
went in the French navy ; one of the few of the old
navy who had remained in France ; a gentleman by
birth, though he had early accepted service under the
Republic, and had, apparently, assumed the Republican
discourtesy of manner and the Napoleonic method of
misrepresenting facts.

Rightly or wrongly, it is certain that Nelson was

strongly prepossessed against him; and his wrath was
extreme when he learned that, in a despatch dated June
15th, 1804, which was published in the *Moniteur*, he had
stated that, having got under way on the 14th and
stood out of the harbour, the English Admiral in the
offing had taken flight; that he had chased him till
nightfall, and that the next morning he was out of sight.
Nelson's description of the incident written at the time
was as follows : " Upon the 14th, M. La Touche came out
with eight sail of the line and six frigates, cut a caper off
Sepet, and went in again. I was off with five ships of
the line, and brought to for his attack, although I did
not believe that anything was meant serious, but merely
a gasconade." He does not appear to have seen the
offensive number of the *Moniteur* till August 8th, when
he wrote to his brother: " I have been expecting M.
La Touche to give me a meeting every day for this year
past, and only hope he will come out before I go
hence. . . . You will have seen his letter of how he
chased me and how I ran. I keep it, and by God, if I
take him he shall eat it." To the Admiralty he wrote
more soberly; but in his familiar letters he gave free
vent to his wrath, and the French Admiral's name is
always borne on a torrent of invective, accompanied
with the expression of a hope to "get a shake at him."
La Touche, however, "gave him the slip " by dying on
August 18th. "He is gone," Nelson wrote as a farewell
shot when the news reached him, "and all his lies with
him." The command of the French fleet devolved on
Rear-Admiral Dumanoir, who after a few weeks was
superseded by Vice-Admiral Villeneuve, an officer of the
old navy who had served under Suffren ; the same who,

in the *Guillaume Tell*, had commanded the rear of the French fleet at the Nile, and for his escape, which, in the judgment of competent persons, betrayed a lamentable want of decision, was considered by Napoleon as born under a fortunate star.

Meantime, Nelson considered it almost certain that the French were meditating a dash at the West Indies. In several letters during September he wrote to the same effect. The Russian force was so strong that it was not likely they would venture eastward. "Suppose this fleet escapes, and gets out of the Straits, I rather think I should bend my course to the westward ; for if they carry seven thousand men—with what they have at Martinique and Guadeloupe—St. Lucia, Grenada, St. Vincent, Antigua, and St. Kitts would fall, and in that case England would be so clamorous for peace that we should humble ourselves. . . . Whatever may be their destination, I shall certainly follow, be it even to the East Indies. Such a pursuit would do more, perhaps, towards restoring me to health than all the doctors."

He was, indeed, by this time longing to be at home again. It would seem that his health was really better during this year than it had been since the repulse at Teneriffe. The shock to his system by the loss of his arm and the excruciating pain which he had afterwards suffered, followed by the severe wound he had received in the Battle of the Nile, was yielding to time ; his position as Commander-in-Chief was all that he could wish ; with Lord Melville he was on perfectly friendly terms ; and it may well be that, as to his domestic relations, his mind was more at ease. What he considered the principal obstacle in the way of his marrying Lady

Hamilton was removed : he probably thought that the difficulty of his being already married might be sur- mounted ; and in any case, time had soothed the irrita- tion of the quarrel, and left him to the happiness which he found in Emma's affection, with, it may be, some- thing of the repose of security and gratified passion. But from time to time a longing for her society returned, and with it the old feeling of ill-health ; "with him," as Stewart wrote in the Baltic, "mind and health invariably sympathised." It was thus that in August, 1804, several of his letters complain of his being ill ; that on the 15th he wrote officially requesting leave of absence for the winter ; he was anxious to serve, and would hope, if allowed, to resume the command in the spring, but at present his "shattered carcase" required rest. The fit, however, happily wore off ; and by October he would seem to have forgotten it, or at any rate, to have preferred his hope of meeting the French fleet at sea.

In his continual quest for intelligence he had all the available Italian and Spanish newspapers regularly sent to him, and Dr. Scott, the chaplain of the *Victory*, who acted as his foreign secretary, read them to him, so far as they contained anything of importance or interest. One day, learning in this manner that a considerable quantity of church-plate was to be sold at Barcelona, he suggested to Scott to go there on a week's leave, and buy some of it for him ; at the same time, perhaps, he might learn something of the public feeling in the place. His desire to have this church-plate seemed curious ; but after he got it the mystery was explained : he had conceived the pretty idea of making a present to the little villages along the north coast of Sardinia, where his ships and fleet had been kindly received. To the church at Maddalena he presented a cross and two candlesticks of silver with a holograph letter, addressed to "The Revd. the Superior of the Church at Maddalena," which ran thus : "*Victory*, October 18th, 1804. REVD. SIR—I have to request that I may be allowed to present to the Church at Maddalena a piece of church-plate as a small token of my esteem for the worthy inhabitants, and of my re-membrance of the hospitable treatment His Majesty's fleet under my command has ever received from them. May God bless us all.—I remain, Revd. Sir, your most obedient servant, NELSON AND BRONTE. The Rev. Dr. Scott will present it to you." This letter, with an Italian translation, presumably by Scott, still hangs, framed and glazed, in the church. It was by such little acts of kindness and consideration that he won the hearts of the people, and obtained their eager and zealous assistance, which might now become of the first importance, as, by the violent seizure of the Spanish treasure-ships off Cape St. Mary's on October 5th, war with Spain was practically commenced, and was formally declared on December 12th.

On January 19th, 1805, Nelson with his little fleet was at Maddalena, when at three o'clock in the after-noon Captain Moubray in the *Active* came in with the news that the French had put to sea the day before ; that he had parted from them at ten o'clock at night abreast of Ajaccio, then steering south with a strong gale at north-west. The fleet immediately prepared for sea, and before six o'clock, with a slight breeze at west-north-

west, ran through the strait between Biche and Sardinia,
and stood to the southward, hoping to meet the enemy
off the south end of Sardinia.   The running through this
strait in the dark,—a "passage so narrow that the ships
could only pass one at a time, each following the stern
lights of its leader,"—has been made the subject of won-
dering admiration by writers ignorant of the sea and of
naval usage, who would seem to have fancied that a
fleet leaving a harbour usually goes out like a herd of
swine crowding through a gateway.   The manœuvre
was one of everyday occurrence, and to a fleet that had
been blockading Toulon for eighteen months was a mere
matter of course.

Nelson, however, had no intelligence as to where
the French were going; but many things concurred to
make him believe they were not, as he had previously
expected, bound out of the Mediterranean.   For a
fortnight the wind had been easterly; they had waited
till it changed to the west, and then put to sea; of that
he was certain.   For some weeks he had information
from trustworthy sources that they were assembling
troops at Toulon, and a body of cavalry; that they had
embarked seven thousand soldiers (which, crowded into
the few ships, eleven sail of the line and some frigates,
precluded the idea of a long voyage), five thousand
saddles, and some field-artillery.   All these seemed to indicate Egypt as their destination; but he did not, as has
been supposed, hurry off to Egypt on a blind impulse.
The persistent westerly gales, and the position he took up
to the south-west of Sardinia, made him certain that,
although the *Active* and *Seahorse* had seen them on the
west of Corsica, they had not passed to the southward

on the west side of Sardinia. He convinced himself
that they had gone neither to Naples nor to Sicily;
they had therefore either put back to Toulon disabled,
or had gone to Egypt. If they had put back disabled,
they were harmless for the time, and it did not matter
whether he was off Toulon or off Alexandria; but if
they had gone to Egypt, clearly they ought to be
followed. So to Egypt he went. As he did not find
them there, he at once returned. At Malta, on February
19th, he learned that they had put back to Toulon in
a very crippled state; but several weeks later, on
March 27th, he still wrote: "The original destination
of the French fleet, I am every day more and more
confirmed, was Egypt."

CHAPTER X

THE fleet was at this time provisioning in the Gulf of Palmas, whence it moved on April 1st to Pula Road at the south end of Sardinia, and sailed on the 3rd, probably with the intention of returning off Toulon; but on the forenoon of the 4th the *Phœbe* joined with the news that the French had again put to sea on March 30th. That Nelson should suppose they were bound for Egypt was natural; but he did not, as has been said, immediately rush off in wild chase of a phantom. "I have covered the channel," he wrote on the 5th, "from Barbary to Toro with frigates and the fleet. The French could not pass before to-day, if this be their route. I must leave as little as possible to chance, and I shall make sure they are to the eastward of me before I risk either Sardinia, Sicily, or Naples; for they may delay their time of coming even this distance, from an expectation that I shall push for Egypt, and thus leave them at liberty to act against Sardinia, Sicily, or Naples." And again on the 7th he wrote: "I must be guided in my further movements by such information as I may be able to obtain; but I shall neither go to the eastward of Sicily or to the westward of Sardinia until I know something positive."

By the 9th he had come to the conclusion that the enemy had gone westward, and endeavoured to follow; but was then met by a persistent westerly wind, against which his progress was necessarily very slow. On the 18th he learned that with a fresh easterly wind they had passed out of the Mediterranean on the 8th, and had been joined by some of the Spanish ships from Cadiz. For him the wind continued "foul, dead foul!" and it was not till May 4th that he anchored at Tetuan, where he watered. On the 6th he went into Gibraltar Bay to provision; but the wind coming easterly, he at once put to sea, with the victuallers in tow, intending to wait off Cape St. Vincent for certain information. On the 9th he anchored in Lagos Bay, where he filled up with provisions; and having, by letters from Lisbon and a personal communication from his friend Captain Campbell of the Portuguese navy, convinced himself that the combined fleet, now numbering eighteen sail of the line, had really gone to the West Indies with the probable intention of attacking Jamaica, he sailed on the 11th in pursuit.

It has been many times repeated, and is very generally believed, that in doing this Nelson was falling into a cunning and deep-laid trap; that he was being decoyed to the West Indies, and was opening the way for an overpowering concentration of force in the Channel, and for a direct invasion of England by the army already assembled at Boulogne; and that this invasion failed to take effect only through the weakness and ineptitude of the French admiral. In such statements there is just enough of known fact to give a plausible appearance of truth to the whole, which is nevertheless wildly

erroneous. It is true that there was an army assembled
at Boulogne; it is probably, and indeed, though it has
been doubted, almost certainly, true that an invasion
of England was intended; it is true that there was a
plan for an overpowering concentration in the Channel;
it is even true that there was a trap; but that Nelson
fell into it is not true; and the assertion that he was
decoyed from European waters is absurd.

In the previous December Napoleon had conceived
a plan for accomplishing his long-threatened invasion
of England, which does not seem to have been generally
understood here, probably because no seaman could have
considered it as feasible. In a few words, it was for
the several fleets to break out of Brest, Rochefort, and
Toulon at nearly the same time; to rendezvous at
Martinique, and returning in a fleet of some fifty sail
of the line, sweep the Channel, and open the way for
the Army of England to cross over. The Rochefort
squadron under Rear-Admiral Missiessy succeeded in
getting to sea on January 11th. Villeneuve, as we have
seen, made the attempt on January 17th, but falling
into bad weather, put back with his fleet disabled, and
did not succeed in getting away till March 30th, only
to find on his arrival at Martinique on May 14th that
Missiessy, having waited the prescribed forty-five days,
had returned to France. Vice-Admiral Ganteaume at
Brest was even less fortunate. The blockade maintained by Cornwallis or Gardner was so close and in
such strength, that he was unable to do more than make
a futile demonstration on April 15th, and return into
the harbour.

But it was not only to join his missing colleagues

that Villeneuve went to Martinique. He, as Missiessy before him, had orders to harass, capture, or destroy such of the English settlements as he could. This was no doubt a feasible operation, which would have profitably occupied the forty days he was directed to wait for Ganteaume ; but it required the command of the sea,— that is, the absence of any force which could meet him on anything like equal terms ; and to ensure this, every effort was made to conceal the destination of the fleet as it sailed from Cadiz, and to mislead Nelson in some other direction. Hence probably the reports which reached Nelson of the embarkation of troops, of cavalry, and of saddles,—all apparently groundless, though some few soldiers were taken on board and landed at Martinique or Guadeloupe. Hence also other reports systematically set on foot by Napoleon, intended to lead Nelson and other squadrons to the East Indies. That Nelson should go to Egypt, and Collingwood, from before Rochefort, should sail for the East Indies, was what Napoleon calculated on. But Nelson's judgment in waiting for definite intelligence before sailing for Egypt rendered one expectation abortive; and the early knowledge which the Admiralty had of Villeneuve's sailing for the West Indies resulted in an order for Collingwood to follow him with an efficient squadron. Collingwood, however, finding that Nelson had already done so, contented himself with sending him a small reinforcement, and with the rest of his squadron keeping watch on the Spanish ships in Cadiz, and preventing them being joined by those at Cartagena. The pursuit of Villeneuve, so far from being what Napoleon had aimed at, utterly spoiled the plan which on paper had looked so neat.

Villeneuve had captured the celebrated Diamond
Rock, and having been joined by two more ships from
France, had sailed from Martinique with the intention
of attacking Antigua or Barbados. On June 8th, however, he learned that Nelson had arrived at Barbados
four days before with fourteen ships. Villeneuve had
been led to believe that Sir Alexander Cochrane was
also at Barbados with five ships of the line ; and not
doubting for a moment that with only twenty ships he
was no match for Nelson with nineteen, he resolved,
and for the only time in his life without hesitation,
to quit the West Indies and return, according to his
instructions, to Ferrol.

Nelson had indeed arrived at Barbados on June 4th,
after a remarkable passage, in which with foul ships,
some of them, especially the *Superb*, scarcely seaworthy,
he had gained twelve days on the allies ; but he brought
with him only ten sail of the line, and had found there
only two more, the other three on the station having
been detained at Jamaica. Still with these twelve he
pushed on at once to look for the enemy. He wished
to go direct to Martinique ; had he done so, he would
in all probability have overtaken Villeneuve under the
lee of Dominica, in almost the very waters where Rodney
had annihilated De Grasse twenty-three years before.
But he was misled by a letter from the Governor of St.
Lucia, with intelligence that the allied fleet had been
seen passing to the southward, and was believed to have
gone to Trinidad. Sir William Myers, the general at
Barbados, offered to accompany him with two thousand soldiers, who were embarked at once, and the fleet
sailed early the next morning. At Trinidad, however,

where he anchored on the 7th, nothing had been seen
of the enemy; and vehemently cursing the false news
and the sender of it, Nelson made sail for Martinique,
where he hoped he might yet find them.   But no fleet
was there; and on the 12th, off Antigua, he learned that
they had passed there four days earlier standing to the
northward.

Concluding that Villeneuve was returning to Europe,
he forthwith despatched the *Curieux* brig with the intelligence to the Admiralty, and, putting into St. John's,
landed Sir William Myers and his two thousand men;
then, on the 13th, having no further news of the enemy's
fleet, he felt confirmed in his conjecture, and followed
under a press of sail.   It was a step which, he felt certain,
neither Villeneuve nor Napoleon would expect; he was
convinced they would suppose him fixed in the West
Indies for a month at least; that he would fear an
attack on Jamaica, and run blindly to leeward to relieve
it.   Napoleon certainly did think so: he took for granted
that Villeneuve, when he heard of Nelson's arrival, would
judge it necessary to leave the West Indies, and that
Nelson, missing him, would run down to Jamaica; but
Napoleon was not a seaman, and did not understand a
seaman's objection to run to leeward until something
more definite than conjecture calls him.   Nelson revolved
all the chances in his mind, and, impressed with the
conviction that Villeneuve had started on his homeward
voyage, lost no time in following.   He believed they
were bound back into the Mediterranean; that they
would go to Toulon; and then, fancying they had
it to themselves, might carry out their design on
Egypt.   He thought that in going to the Medi-

terranean, as in going to the West Indies, they were
trying to evade him, but the theory of a decoy did
not occur to him. He was appointed to keep watch on
the Toulon fleet, and to do so involved following it
wherever it went, till he could catch and annihilate it.
So he now steered for the Straits of Gibraltar, knowing
that he would at any rate learn whether Villeneuve had
passed, if indeed he did not hear of him or come up with
him on the way.

On July 18th he joined Collingwood off Cadiz, but
neither he nor Collingwood had seen or heard anything
of the French fleet. Nelson had already seen the possibility of Villeneuve making for Ferrol, and four days
after leaving Antigua had despatched a warning note to
the captains of any ships cruising off the Western Islands,
strongly recommending them to proceed at once towards Ferrol, to give the information to the admiral
commanding off that port. This seems to have escaped
notice ; and it has been stated that Nelson, so engrossed
in the idea of Egypt, could not entertain any idea of
the French fleet going anywhere else than to the Straits ;
while Collingwood, with a more logical mind and a
keener perception, at once saw what was intended. Such
an opinion is altogether at variance with the fact. What
Collingwood wrote on July 19th, after hearing Nelson's
surmises and knowing that the enemy had not come to
Gibraltar, was that they had probably gone to Ferrol,
and intended to go to Ireland. In such a guess there
was no particular sagacity. Nelson had already suggested to him that they had gone to Ferrol : long before
they escaped from Toulon he had suggested that they
might attempt to push for Ireland ; and if at the pre-

sent time he did not mention Ireland, it may have been
that his information showed him that the state of affairs
in Ireland was not such as to encourage the attempt at
that time.

However that may have been, the fact remains that
Collingwood's guess, so far as it was his, was altogether
wrong; that Nelson's was altogether right.   The French
not only did not attempt the invasion of Ireland,
which Collingwood considered "the real mark and butt
of all their operations"; but from first to last during
this campaign they had no intention of doing so.
Nelson's calculation that if they did not come to the
Straits they would go to Ferrol, was exactly what they
were ordered to do.   Of their further operations he
said nothing; it may be that after the warning he had
despatched on June 17th, he thought that if they got
to Ferrol at all they might not care to quit it again; it
may be that his expression, "Gone to the northward,"
implied an endeavour to join the Brest fleet, as to their
doing which he might think his old friend Cornwallis
would have a word to say.

On July 19th the fleet anchored at Gibraltar, and on
the 20th Nelson noted in his diary that he went on
shore for the first time since June 16th, 1803; and
that he had not set foot out of the *Victory* for two years
all but ten days.

Meanwhile the *Curieux*, pursuing her voyage under
a press of sail, sighted and passed the French fleet, noting
that they were steering a more northerly course than
for Cadiz; on arriving in England therefore on July 8th,
Bettesworth was able to say with some certainty that
they would make the land near Cape Finisterre.   Acting

on this information, the Admiralty at once sent orders for the squadrons before Rochefort and Ferrol to unite and look out for them some thirty or forty leagues to the westward. The fleet of fifteen sail of the line, thus collected under the command of Rear-Admiral Sir Robert Calder, met Villeneuve with his twenty ships on July 22nd. The weather was hazy, almost foggy; and the French, being to windward, were able to avoid a close action. A partial encounter, however, took place, as the result of which two of the Spanish ships were captured. The fleets continued in sight of each other during the 23rd and 24th, but there was no further fighting, and on the 28th Villeneuve anchored at Vigo. His fleet was short of provisions and water; a great many men were sick; several of the ships had received a good deal of damage on the 22nd, and three of them were not in a state to keep the sea. But Nelson had no intelligence of his movements until July 25th, when he learned that on June 19th the *Curieux* had seen the combined fleet standing on a more northerly course. Acting on this he proceeded northward, sending on word to Cornwallis that he was on his way to join him. He did actually join him on August 15th with eleven sail of the line, and, on an order from Cornwallis, went on in the *Victory* to Spithead, where he anchored on the 18th. The next day he struck his flag and went to Merton, where he passed the next few weeks.

It would appear then that, according to the idea so often formulated, it was during the three weeks immediately preceding August 15th that England was exposed to such imminent danger in consequence of Nelson's having been decoyed to the West Indies.

The dates have therefore a peculiar importance. We have seen that it was July 28th before Villeneuve could reach Vigo, and then in such a distressed condition that for the moment he could do nothing but try, on the 31st, to reach Ferrol. Napoleon had, however, sent orders that on no account was he to go into Ferrol; therefore, being unable to keep the sea, he went into Corunna, where he refitted as well as the resources of the place allowed; and, having been joined by the squadron in Ferrol, he put to sea on August 13th, with instructions to proceed off Brest, where Napoleon still hoped he might effect a junction with Ganteaume. He had with him at this time twenty-nine sail of the line. The five ships from Rochefort had also put to sea, intending to join him off Ferrol. He sent the *Didon*, a 44-gun frigate, to give them orders to join him off Brest; but the *Didon* was met on the way by the English 40-gun frigate *Phœnix*, and was captured after a sharp action; the Rochefort squadron did not therefore get the orders intended for it, and had no further share in the campaign.

Whether, if Villeneuve had in accordance with his instructions come off Brest, he would have been able to effect a junction with Ganteaume, must seem very doubtful. After being reinforced by a great part of Nelson's squadron, Cornwallis had also been joined by most of Calder's, and had under his command a fleet of thirty-five ships of the line, in face of which the proposed junction might have been difficult or impossible. Villeneuve had, in fact, so clearly realised this, that when on August 15th he saw, in the north-eastern quarter, three ships (which were afterwards known to be the *Phœnix*, with her prize, in convoy of the 74-gun ship *Dragon*), and learned from a neutral merchant-ship that they were a detachment of an English fleet of twenty-five sail, he did not wait to investigate the intelligence, which was entirely false, but at once decided that the object of his voyage could not be carried out; and, without attempting it further, turned southward and went to Cadiz, his advanced ships chasing away the small squadron which, under Collingwood, was watching off the port. He anchored in the harbour of Cadiz on August 17th.

Collingwood at once sent the important news to England in the *Euryalus* frigate. She arrived at Spithead on September 1st; and on the 2nd, at five o'clock in the morning, Captain Blackwood called at Merton, where he found Nelson already up and dressed. Immediately on seeing him Nelson exclaimed, "I am sure you bring me news of the French and Spanish fleets, and I think I shall yet have to beat them." A few hours later Nelson followed him to London, and in talking over the operations that were intended on his return to the Mediterranean, he repeated, "Depend upon it, Blackwood, I shall yet give Mr. Villeneuve a drubbing."

The story, as afterwards told by Harrison, that Nelson was unwilling to leave Merton, and yielded only to the persuasions of Lady Hamilton, exclaiming, "If there were more Emmas there would be more Nelsons," is only one of the many lies with a purpose which Lady Hamilton put in circulation in order to strengthen the claims which she fancied she had on the Government. Southey, ignorantly or inconsiderately, gave it a currency which it could not otherwise have had, and it has thus been very commonly received as absolute fact. It is, on the contrary, absolute falsehood. It is indeed possible that Nelson may have uttered some endearing expressions of regret at having to quit his loved companion, but it is quite certain that it had been already arranged that he was to resume the command; the determination of the time had been left to M. Villeneuve, and it was now resolved that he should go out at once in the *Victory.* Other ships should follow as fast as they could be got ready. During the fortnight immediately preceding as well as subsequent to September 2nd, Nelson was repeatedly at the Admiralty and the office of the Secretary of State. In one of his visits to this latter he met, for the only time, the Duke of Wellington, then Sir Arthur Wellesley, who used in after years to give a lively account of the conversation, and of the double estimate of Nelson which he formed from it; of Nelson as a vapouring and vainglorious charlatan, and of Nelson as a well-informed officer and statesman, "really a very superior man." There is, in fact, abundant evidence that Nelson not infrequently displayed the unblushing and self-asserting vanity of a child, with all a child's love of praise and a woman's love of flattery, and that Lady Hamilton used to administer both to him in abundance. That Nelson could, on occasion, act as an officer and judge as a statesman, we knew before the Duke's story was made public.

CHAPTER XI

TRAFALGAR

ON September 13th Nelson finally left home. For that day he noted in his diary: "At half-past ten drove from dear, dear Merton, where I left all which I hold dear in this world, to go and serve my King and country. May the great God whom I adore enable me to fulfil the expectations of my country; and if it is His good pleasure that I should return, my thanks will never cease being offered up to the throne of His mercy. If it is His good providence to cut short my days upon earth, I bow with the greatest submission, relying that He will protect those so dear to me that I may leave behind. His will be done. Amen."

The next morning at six o'clock he arrived at Portsmouth, and at two, after being followed through the streets by an adoring crowd, he embarked at the bathing-machines. The spot pointed out by local tradition is a few yards to the west of the old Southsea pier, immediately below the Assembly Rooms. Canning and George Rose accompanied him on board and dined with him. Early the next morning, Sunday, September 15th, the *Victory* sailed with the *Euryalus* in company.

Meantime the squadron off Cadiz was being largely reinforced. Sir Richard Bickerton from the Mediterranean and Calder from the Bay of Biscay had joined Collingwood, bringing his numbers up to twenty-four ships of the line. To the several captains the service seemed merely the beginning of another interminable blockade, more irksome, more dreary, than any yet undertaken; for Collingwood was not a sympathetic commander, and finding his sole happiness in fond visions of home, he took no measures to alleviate the severity of the work. No visiting was allowed except on strict duty. Collingwood neither entertained himself nor permitted others to entertain. Country vessels from the African coast came into the fleet almost daily with fruit, vegetables, or live-stock ; but the boats could not be hoisted out, and the fruit or vegetables could not be bought. In the familiar letters which Captain Codrington (then commanding the *Orion*, and twenty-two years later, as Sir Edward Codrington, Commander-in-Chief at Navarino) wrote to his wife, we have the state of things most clearly explained. "Is Lord Nelson coming to us ?" he wrote. "I anxiously hope he may be, that I may once in my life see a Commander-in-Chief endeavouring to make a hard and disagreeable service as palatable to those serving under him as circumstances will admit of, and keeping up, by his example, that animation so necessary for such an occasion. For charity's sake send us Lord Nelson, ye men of power !"

The men of power had granted the prayer before it was uttered. Nelson, in the *Victory*, joined the fleet on September 28th, having sent on the *Euryalus* to announce his coming, and with an order to Collingwood

neither to fire a salute nor hoist the colours. " It is as
well," he wrote, "not to proclaim to the enemy every
ship which may join the fleet."   But if no official compliments were allowed, he was received with heartfelt
rejoicing by those who had been groaning under the
dismal rule of his predecessor.   " Lord Nelson is
arrived," wrote Codrington on the 29th ; " a sort of
general joy has been the consequence, and many good
effects will arise from our change of system.   He joined
us too late yesterday for communication.   I had not got
any of your letters before I waited on Lord Nelson this
morning.   He received me in an easy, polite manner,
and on giving me your letter said that, being entrusted
with it by a lady, he made a point of delivering it himself " ; and the next day : " The signal has been made
this morning for all of us who did not dine on board the
Victory yesterday to go there to-day.   What our late
chief will think of this, I don't know ; but I well know
what the fleet will think of the difference ; and even
you, our good wives, who have some causes of disap-
probation, will allow the superiority of Nelson in all
those social arrangements which bind his captains to
their Admiral.   The signal is made that boats may be
hoisted out to buy fruit, stock, or anything from vessels
coming into the fleet.   This, I trust, will be a common
signal hereafter, but it is the first day I have seen it
made."   Codrington had not been with Nelson before ;
he met him as a perfect stranger, and within two days
was his devoted servant.   The delicate attention about
his wife's letter had captivated him ; the invitation to a
pleasant dinner had won him ; the being treated as a
man, a brother, and a dear friend enthralled him.   So

it was with every one who came under the fascination
of Nelson's genial manner ; and the service was strengthened by the duty being performed with goodwill and
the utmost of each man's soul, instead of grudgingly,
with hate in the heart and fear of a court-martial before
the eyes.

The retreat of Villeneuve to Cadiz put an end, for
the moment, to Bonaparte's hopes of obtaining the command of the Channel and of being able to cross over to
England.   He had already been anxiously considering
the state of affairs in Germany, where the alliance of
Austria, Prussia, and Russia rendered his presence
necessary ; and now, understanding that it was impossible at that time to pursue his schemes for the invasion
of England, he determined to let them rest for the
present, and take them up again when he had demo-
lished this threatening coalition.   He accordingly broke
up the camp at Boulogne on September 2nd, and led
his army into Germany for one of his most brilliant
campaigns.   At the same time he sent Villeneuve orders
to leave Cadiz and return to Toulon after ranging along
the coast of Italy.   Of the effective numbers of the fleet
with Villeneuve he knew little : of those of the English
fleet off Cadiz he knew less ; and by repeated insulting
messages to Villeneuve, and by threats to supersede him
from the command if he did not immediately put to sea,
he at last compelled him to do so.

From the day of his joining the fleet Nelson had
endeavoured, by keeping out of sight of land, to deceive
the French Admiral as to the English force.   It appears,
however, that Villeneuve was fairly well informed on
this point, that he had a correct knowledge of the

general movements of the fleet, and that when, on October 3rd, Nelson detached Rear-Admiral Louis with six ships to fill up with provisions and water at Gibraltar and Tetuan, he was acquainted with their absence; on the 18th he received intelligence of their being at Gibraltar. Previous to parting company, Louis, whose flag was flying on board the *Canopus*, dined with Nelson, and on taking leave said, " You are sending us away, my Lord—the enemy will come out and we shall have no share in the battle." Nelson replied, " My dear Louis, I have no other means of keeping my fleet complete in provisions and water but by sending them in detachments to Gibraltar. The enemy will come out and we shall fight them, but there will be time for you to get back first. I look upon *Canopus* as my right hand, and I send you first to ensure your being here to help to beat them." He was, in fact, trusting to the secrecy of the ocean, and calculated that, though the stoppage of the coasting-trade and the strict prevention of supplies reaching Cadiz by sea must eventually force the allied fleet out, there had not yet been time for the blockade to make itself seriously felt. But Villeneuve, on receiving the news from Gibraltar, judged that the opportunity was as favourable as any at all likely to occur, and on the 19th he began to unmoor. Some of his ships got outside that same evening, others not till the next day; by the afternoon of the 20th he was fairly at sea, with thirty-three ships of the line besides frigates, and steering at first towards the west with a southerly wind, but later on towards the south-east with the wind very light at south-west.

The English fleet at this time consisted of twenty-

seven ships of the line of battle, and on the afternoon of
the 19th was, for the most part, with Nelson about
sixteen leagues west-south-west from Cadiz, but connected
with the shore by a line of ships and frigates, which kept
him constantly informed of the movements of the enemy.
It was thus at once signalled to him that the allied fleet
was coming out of harbour; and supposing, as was the
case, that Villeneuve wished to enter the Mediterranean,
he stood towards the Straits' mouth.   At daybreak on
the 20th the enemy was not in sight, and the fleet continued under easy sail, standing towards the north
during the day, and back again towards the south
during the night.   At four o'clock on the morning of
the 21st it wore towards the north; and at daylight,
Cape Trafalgar then bearing east by south, distant seven
leagues, the enemy's fleet was seen on the same line of
bearing, distant about ten or twelve miles.

During the weeks of his watch on Cadiz, Nelson had
been urging the necessity of sending him more ships.
After Louis had gone to Gibraltar he had but twenty-
three, while the enemy had thirty-six actually in the
port.   "Should they come out," he wrote to the First
Lord of the Admiralty on October 5th, "I shall immediately bring them to battle; but though I should not
doubt of spoiling any voyage they may attempt, yet I
hope for the arrival of the ships from England, that as
an enemy's fleet they may be annihilated."   And the
next day, in a private letter, he said: "It is annihilation
that the country wants, and not merely a splendid
victory of twenty-three to thirty-six—honourable to the
parties concerned, but absolutely useless in the extended
scale to bring Bonaparte to his marrow-bones.   Numbers

can only annihilate; therefore I hope the Admiralty
will send the fixed force as soon as possible."

He thought it probable that, by the junction of the
Rochefort and Cartagena squadrons, the allies would be
able to put forty-six ships in their line of battle, and he
hoped that the return of Louis and fresh reinforcements
would give him not less than forty. It was in this
expectation that he drew up the celebrated memorandum
which he issued to the fleet on October 9th. In it he said
that, thinking it almost impossible under varying conditions of wind and weather to form a fleet of forty
ships in line of battle without such loss of time as would
probably cause also the loss of the opportunity of bringing the enemy to action, he had resolved to keep the
fleet in its order of sailing. The order of sailing was to
be the order of battle; and this order of sailing was
prescribed as in two lines of sixteen ships each, with an
advanced squadron of eight of the fastest two-deckers,
ready to "make a line of twenty-four sail on whichever
line he might direct." He then went on to consider the
possible circumstances of the battle, according as the
enemy should be to windward or to leeward; but in
each case the dominant idea was that the lee line,
under Collingwood, should concentrate its attack on
the twelve ships in the enemy's rear, while he himself, with the weather line and the advanced squadron,
should overawe the enemy's van and fall on their
centre; so that, when the battle was fairly joined, the
whole forty of the English ships should be clustered
on about twenty-six of the enemy. It was most distinctly laid down that the lee line was to begin the
action, and that his own first care would be to pre-

vent the enemy's van interfering with the attack on
their rear.

No clearer exposition of tactical principles was ever
penned ; and though, under the force of circumstances,
some of the details prescribed in the memorandum were
departed from, the leading idea of crushing the enemy's
rear with the lee line, and overawing the enemy's van
with the weather line, was very exactly adhered to.
Between October 9th and 21st, not only Collingwood,
but Rear-Admiral Lord Northesk, who commanded in
the third post, and the several captains of the fleet were
in frequent intercourse with the Commander-in-Chief,
and the meaning and spirit of the memorandum were
explained and discussed in a friendly manner by word
of mouth ; so that on the morning of the 21st, when
the enemy's fleet was in sight, every officer in command
of a ship knew precisely what to expect and what to do.
The necessity for many signals was thus entirely done
away with, and, so far as ordering the battle was concerned, only three were made, and those within a
few minutes of first sighting the enemy's fleet. They
were : (1) "Form order of sailing in two columns."
(2) "Prepare for battle." (3) "Bear up (in succession)
and sail large on the course steered by the Admiral."

The wind was very light at about west-north-west,
and as the *Victory* led the way towards the enemy she
made all possible sail. The other ships did the same,
and the advance to the attack thus became more like
a trial of rates of sailing than a formation in precise
lines. The lines were, indeed, very irregular ; and
some of the ships, which had been thrown forward as
look-outs, as the *Africa*, or were at a distance from the

main body of the fleet, as the *Prince*, never got into the lines at all.

On the evening of the 20th Villeneuve had formed his fleet in line of battle, heads to the southward, with a reserve squadron to windward. The signal guns and rockets of the English during the night kept him aware of their immediate neighbourhood ; and at daylight on the 21st, with their fleet in sight, he repeated the signal for the line of battle on the starboard tack. On this the reserve squadron took its station in the van, the Spanish Admiral, Gravina, himself leading, with his flag on board the *Principe de Asturias*, of 112 guns. As the English advanced, and he saw that in the very light breeze it was impossible to avoid fighting, Villeneuve judged it prudent to lay his ships' heads in the direction of Cadiz, and a little after eight made the signal to wear all together and form line of battle on the port tack. The extreme lightness of the wind, the unskilfulness of the officers, and the want of training and seamanship in his ships' companies, rendered the manoeuvre very long. It was not till after ten o'clock that the fleet was formed on the other tack, and then most irregularly, the ships being in some places crowded together, with two or even three abreast, in others separated by wide intervals, and the whole line sagging away to leeward, so as to present a deep crescent rather than any near approach to the ideal line of battle. It is thus impossible to give the exact order of the enemy's ships ; but, as nearly as can be, it was the following.

Ship.		Guns.	Result of the Battle.
1. *Neptuno*	S	80	Captured ; recaptured Oct. 23
2. *Scipion*	F	74	Captured Nov. 4 ; sent home
3. *Intrépide*	F	74	Captured ; burnt
4. *Formidable*	F	80	(Rear-Admiral Dumanoir le Pelley) Captured Nov. 4 ; sent home
5. *Rayo*	S	100	Captured on Oct. 24 ; wrecked
6. *Duguay-Trouin*	F	74	Captured Nov. 4 ; sent home
7. *Mont-Blanc*	F	74	Captured Nov. 4 ; sent home
8. *San Francisco de Assisi*	S	74	Wrecked on Oct. 23
9. *San Augustino*	S	74	Captured ; burnt
10. *Héros*	F	74	Escaped into Cadiz
11. *Santisima Trinidad*	S	130	(Rear-Admiral Cisneros) Captured ; foundered
12. *Bucentaure*	F	80	(Vice-Admiral Villeneuve) Captured ; wrecked
13. *Neptune*	F	80	Escaped into Cadiz
14. *Redoutable*	F	74	Captured ; foundered
15. *San Leandro*	S	64	Escaped into Cadiz
16. *San Justo*	S	74	Escaped into Cadiz
17. *Indomptable*	F	80	Wrecked on Oct. 24
18. *Santa Ana*	S	112	(Vice-Admiral Alava) Captured ; recaptured on Oct. 23
19. *Fougueux*	F	74	Captured ; wrecked
20. *Monarca*	S	74	Captured ; wrecked
21. *Pluton*	F	74	Escaped into Cadiz
22. *Algésiras*	F	74	(Rear-Admiral Magon) Captured ; retaken by crew
23. *Bahama*	S	74	Captured ; taken to Gibraltar
24. *Aigle*	F	74	Captured ; wrecked
25. *Swiftsure*	F	74	Captured ; taken to Gibraltar
26. *Argonaute*	F	74	Escaped into Cadiz
27. *Montañes*	S	74	Escaped into Cadiz
28. *Argonauta*	S	80	Captured ; scuttled
29. *Berwick*	F	74	Captured ; wrecked
30. *San Juan Nepomuceno*	S	74	Captured ; taken to Gibraltar
31. *San Ildefonso*	S	74	Captured ; taken to Gibraltar
32. *Achille*	F	74	Caught fire and blew up
33. *Principe de Asturias*	S	112	(Vice-Admiral Gravina) Escaped into Cadiz

Five frigates, *Cornélie, Hermione, Hortense, Rhin, Thémis*, and the brigs *Argus* and *Furet*, all French, were ranged on the lee side of the line, at some distance, and had no part in the action.

Similarly, though from a different reason, as already explained, the order of the English ships cannot be exactly given, though, with some exceptions, the following is something like it.

WEATHER LINE.

Ship.	Guns.	Captain.	Loss in the Battle.		
			K.	W.	Total.
1. *Victory*	100	T. M. Hardy (Vice - Admiral Lord Nelson— killed)	57	102	159
2. *Téméraire*	98	E. Harvey	47	76	123
3. *Neptune*	98	T. F. Fremantle	10	34	44
4. *Leviathan*	74	H. W. Bayntun	4	22	26
5. *Conqueror*	74	Israel Pellew	3	9	12
6. *Britannia*	100	C. Bullen (Rear - Admiral Lord Northesk)	10	42	52
7. *Agamemnon*	64	Sir E. Berry	2	8	10
8. *Ajax*	74	Lieut. J. Pilfold	2	9	11
9. *Orion*	74	E. Codrington	1	23	24
10. *Minotaur*	74	C. J. M. Mansfield	3	22	25
11. *Spartiate*	74	Sir F. Laforey	3	20	23
12. (*Africa*)	64	H. Digby	18	44	62
		Carried forward	160	411	571

LEE LINE.

Ship.	Guns.	Captain.	Loss in the Battle.		
			K.	W.	Total.
		Brought forward	160	411	571
1. *Royal Sove-reign*	100	E. Rotheram (Vice - Admiral Collingwood)	47	94	141
2. *Belleisle*	74	W. Hargood	33	93	126
3. *Mars*	74	G. Duff—killed	29	69	98
4. *Tonnant*	80	C. Tyler	26	50	76
5. *Bellerophon*	74	J. Cooke—killed	27	123	150
6. *Colossus*	74	J. N. Morris	40	160	200
7. *Achille*	74	R. King	13	59	72
8. *Dreadnought*	98	J. Conn	7	26	33
9. *Polyphemus*	64	R. Redmill	2	4	6
10. *Revenge*	74	R. Moorsom	28	51	79
11. *Swiftsure*	74	W. G. Rutherford	9	8	17
12. *Defiance*	74	P. C. Durham	17	53	70
13. *Thunderer*	74	Lieut. J. Stock-ham	4	12	16
14. (*Prince*)	98	R. Grindall	...	...	...
15. *Defence*	74	G. Hope	7	29	36
		Total	449	1242	1691

The frigates *Euryalus* (Captain H. Blackwood), *Naiad* (T. Dundas), *Phœbe* (T. B. Capel, and *Sirius* (W. Prowse), with the schooner *Pickle* (Lieut. J. R. Lapenotiere), and cutter *Entreprenante* (Lieut. R. B. Young), were present to windward of the weather column, but took no part in the battle.

It had been laid down by Lord Nelson in his memorandum of October 9th, that, if the fleet should be to windward of the enemy, it would be his aim to bring it, in three lines, parallel to and within gunshot of the enemy ; from which position the lee line would bear up all together and fall on the enemy's rear, while the weather line and advance squadron threatened the van, until such time as it seemed expedient for them also to bear up and fall on the enemy's centre. The extreme lightness of the wind, however, rendered it quite impossible to get into the prescribed position without risking the loss of the whole day and of the opportunity to engage at all. This contingency had no doubt been discussed by Nelson in the days preceding the battle, so that the modification in the Admiral's plan was at once understood. Ideally, the English fleet was in two lines perpendicular to the enemy's one line; actually, the lines on both sides were extremely irregular, and on the part of the English were rather elongated clusters.

Having thus seen all things arranged as was best suited to the circumstances, Nelson went down to his cabin and entered in his diary a brief note of the occurrences of the morning. Then, on his knees, he added :—" May the great God whom I worship grant to my country and for the benefit of Europe in general a great and glorious victory ; and may no misconduct in any one tarnish it ; and may humanity after victory be the predominant feature in the British fleet. For myself, individually, I commit my life to Him who made me, and may His blessing light upon my endeavours for serving my country faithfully. To Him I resign myself and the just cause which is intrusted to me to defend."

He afterwards wrote, or at any rate signed, in the presence of Blackwood and Hardy, that remarkable document which has been called the codicil to his will, in which he briefly stated the services which, as he had been led to believe, Lady Hamilton had rendered to the country. She had obtained, he said, in 1796 the King of Spain's letter to the King of Naples acquaint-

ing him of his intention to declare war against
England, and had thus been able to give timely
warning to the English Ministry ; and in 1798, she had,
by her " influence with the Queen of Naples, caused
letters to be wrote to the Governor of Syracuse, that he
was to encourage the fleet being supplied with everything, should they put into any port in Sicily."   As it
had not been in his power to reward these services, " I
leave," he wrote, " Emma, Lady Hamilton, a legacy to
my King and country, that they will give her an ample
provision to maintain her rank in life.   I also leave to
the beneficence of my country my adopted daughter,
Horatia Nelson Thompson ; and I desire she will use in
future the name of Nelson only.   These are the only
favours I ask of my King and country at this moment
when I am going to fight their battle."

The approach towards the enemy's line was necessarily slow ; at first it was not more than three knots an
hour, and as the breeze got lighter even this rate was
lessened.   About eleven o'clock, the fleets being then
little more than two miles apart, Nelson, rightly inter-
preting the manœuvre which the combined fleet had so
clumsily executed, telegraphed to Collingwood, " I
intend to push through the enemy's line to prevent
them from getting into Cadiz " ; and half an hour later
he made the celebrated signal, " ENGLAND EXPECTS
THAT EVERY MAN WILL DO HIS DUTY."   It is said
that, as he saw the flags going up, Collingwood
remarked half-peevishly to his flag-lieutenant, " I
wish Nelson would make no more signals ; we all understand what we have to do."   When, however, the signal
was reported, he was delighted, and ordered it to be

announced to the ship's company, by whom it was
received with the greatest enthusiasm. On board most
of the ships of the fleet it was similarly announced and
similarly received; but in some the captains thought it
unnecessary, and nothing was said about it.

The modification of the plan of attack, which the circumstances of the weather had rendered necessary, was
not allowed to affect the essential part of it. Collingwood, at the head of the lee line, was still to lead
through the enemy's rear; Nelson, at the head of the
weather line, was still to take care that Collingwood was
not interrupted. It was thus not by accident, nor by
better sailing, nor by more careful trimming of sails,
to all of which it has been assigned, but in accordance
with the prearranged plan, that the *Royal Sovereign* was
considerably ahead of the *Victory* as, closely followed
by the *Belleisle, Mars, Tonnant*, and the rest, she steered
straight for the rear division of the combined fleet. It
was about noon when she entered between the horns of
the crescent, bringing the enemy's van and rear equally
abaft the beam. Immediately in front of her was the
Santa Ana, with the flag of Vice-Admiral Alava, close
astern of which was the *Fougueux*. The *San Leandro,
San Justo*, and *Indomptable* ought to have been ahead of
the *Santa Ana ;* but they had fallen considerably to leeward, and their guns were thus to a great extent masked
by the *Santa Ana* herself, when the Spanish Vice-
Admiral opened his fire on the *Royal Sovereign*.

His doing so was the signal for the ships of both
fleets to hoist their colours, the English all flying the
white ensign, to avoid the confusion which Nelson
thought might arise from the use of different flags ; for

while he himself was Vice-Admiral and Lord Northesk
Rear-Admiral of the White, Collingwood was Vice-
Admiral of the Blue.   In addition to the ensign, each
ship flew two or more union-jacks in different parts
of the rigging.   The Admirals wore their proper flags ;
and at the *Victory's* maintopgallant mast-head was the
signal, "Engage the enemy more closely."

The advance of the English ships had by this time
become extremely slow, and for full twenty minutes the
Royal Sovereign was under the direct fire of the *Santa
Ana* and *Fougueux*, and more partially under that of
four or five other ships.   She ought to have been beaten
into matches, but so bad was the enemy's gunnery
practice that she sustained no loss of any importance ;
none at all, indeed, beyond what drew from Collingwood
the sorrowing cry : "Oh dear, oh dear ! I forgot to shift
that new foretopsail.   It won't be worth anything after
this."   But about twenty minutes after noon she passed
slowly under the stern of the *Santa Ana* across the
bows of the *Fougueux.*   The first gun she fired was a
68-pounder carronade on the port side of the forecastle.
This was loaded with one round shot and a keg of five
hundred musket-bullets, and was now discharged slap
into the stern of the *Santa Ana.*   A second or two later
the starboard carronade, loaded in the same way, was
discharged into the bows of the *Fougueux.*   In slow
succession, each gun as it bore, all loaded with two round
shot, some with three, was fired into the stern of the
Santa Ana or the bows of the *Fougueux.*   As she drew
clear, the *Royal Sovereign's* helm was put hard a-starboard
and she shot up alongside of the *Santa Ana,* where she
engaged her broadside to broadside, at the distance of

only a few yards. In this position, however, she was exposed to the fire of the *San Leandro*, *San Justo*, *Indomptable* and *Fougueux ;* but, whether from their fear of hitting the *Santa Ana* or from the actual badness of their gunnery, her loss, though severe, was nothing like so great as might have been expected. In a few minutes the *Belleisle* took the extreme pressure off her : hauling up a little as she passed under the *Santa Ana's* stern, she fired her port broadside into the Spaniard's starboard quarter ; a minute or two later she passed close under the stern of the *Indomptable*, raking her with terrible effect, and on the *Indomptable's* hastily bearing up, she engaged the *Fougueux*, and afterwards the *Aigle*, *Achille*, and *Neptune*. A reference to the original positions of these three ships will show how extreme was the confusion in the allies' line of battle. Still the *Belleisle* suffered most severely, losing all three masts and bowsprit and one hundred and twenty - six men killed and wounded.

Meantime Nelson, with the weather line, was occupied in providing that Collingwood should not be interrupted. He thought it not improbable that, so soon as the plan of the English attack was seen and understood, the allies' van might wear to the assistance of the centre and rear ; and accordingly, as he approached their line, he hauled up a little as though intending to range along and attack the van. Rear-Admiral Dumanoir, commanding the head of the enemy's line, so interpreted the manœuvre, or, at least, said that he did ; though, as the enemy's line was by the wind, and the *Victory* never took in her studding-sails, it is difficult to understand how he could have been deceived by the very palpable feint. All that

Nelson wished, however, was gained ; and, keeping away again, he steered for the centre of the line.

Here was the huge *Santisima Trinidad* of 130 guns, commonly spoken of as a four-decker. She was, in fact, a three-decker, with guns along the gangways ; but was by far the largest ship then afloat. She was, however, a Spaniard, and carried only a rear-admiral's flag. Nelson was anxious to match himself against Villeneuve, who, he was convinced, was near the centre ; but among the number of tricolours displayed Villeneuve's flag could not be made out, and chance, rather than judgment, determined the place through which the *Victory* passed. Captain Hardy represented to Nelson that the enemy's ships were so crowded at the point abreast them that it was impossible to go through without fouling some one or other. "It does not signify which we run on board of," answered Nelson. "Go on board which you please ; take your choice."

The *Victory* had all this time been sustaining the fire of the *Bucentaure*, *Santisima Trinidad*, and the ships ahead and astern of these. When yet nearly a mile distant, the *Bucentaure* fired a trial shot, which fell short ; a few minutes later another, and then others, till at last, one going through the *Victory's* main-topgallant sail, gave the enemy a visible proof that their shot would reach. Then every ship that could bring a gun to bear opened fire. But though they made a great deal of noise and smoke, and though the shot fell thick all around, comparatively few struck the *Victory*, which on her part reserved her fire, though one or two of her foremost guns were discharged accidentally, or without orders. For nearly half an hour she was exposed to this heavy

Q

fire. The secretary, Dr. Scott, standing by Nelson's side, was killed by a round-shot; another passed between Nelson and Captain Hardy. A double-headed shot swept away eight marines drawn up on the poop; the rest were immediately ordered down, and dispersed round the ship. The mizen-topmast was shot away about two-thirds of the way up; the fore-sail and fore-topsail were in ribbons; the wheel was knocked to pieces. But this, with some fifty men in all killed or wounded, was the full amount of loss sustained by the *Victory* from this tremendous cannonade.

At last, a little before one, she passed under the stern of the *Bucentaure*, so close that her main yard-arm fouled the *Bucentaure's* vangs. Her fire was delivered in exactly the same way as the *Royal Sovereign's*. The 68-pounder carronade on the port side of the forecastle was the first gun, and its charge of a round-shot and a keg of five hundred musket-bullets was discharged into the *Bucentaure's* cabin windows. As she slowly moved ahead, every one of the fifty guns on her broadside, all double, some treble shotted, was deliberately discharged in the same manner. It was said afterwards by the *Bucentaure's* officers that twenty of her guns were dismounted and nearly four hundred of her men killed or wounded by this one terrible broadside.

On the other hand, the moment the *Victory's* bows opened clear of the *Bucentaure's* stern, she was exposed to the direct fire of the *Neptune* and *Redoutable*. But this, however well intended, was harmless in comparison with the *Victory's*; and though at such a short distance it was impossible to help sometimes hitting such a huge target as a three-decker, the greater number of the shot were scattered about through her rigging, and but few struck the hull or caused any loss to the crew. It was probably Hardy's intention, after drawing clear of the *Bucentaure*, to range up on her starboard beam, as the *Royal Sovereign* had done to the *Santa Ana*. If so, however, he was unable to execute it; for the *Redoutable* had closed up to such a degree that, whether accidentally or of set purpose, the two ships fell foul of each other, the starboard bow of the *Victory* striking the port bow of the *Redoutable;* and her foreyard catching in the *Redoutable's* rigging, the two ships fell alongside each other and so remained.

The steady fire from the *Victory's* lower and middle decks drove the *Redoutable's* men from their guns; but above, the advantage was with the French. Nelson, who had twice seen a French ship destroyed by fire, was keenly sensible of the danger of combustibles in the tops, and had strictly forbidden their use. The *Victory's* tops were thus unarmed; those of the *Redoutable*, on the contrary, were full of men, and their musketry and coehorns cleared the *Victory's* forecastle and upper deck. This gave the Frenchmen the idea of boarding and possibly capturing the *Victory*, thus taken at a disadvantage; but seeing them crowding in the gangway, Mr. Wilmot, the boatswain of the *Victory*, fired the starboard forecastle carronade into the thick of them. Loaded as the other had been, it caused terrible havoc, and for the moment they fell back. The musketry fire from the *Redoutable's* tops, however, continued; and about twenty minutes past one a chance shot from her mizen-top struck Nelson on the left shoulder as he stood near the hatchway, facing aft. The bullet passed down through the epaulette, through the lungs, through the spine, and lodged in the muscles of the back. He fell, on the very same spot where his secretary had been killed shortly before. As Captain Hardy attempted to raise him, he said, "They've done for me at last, Hardy." "I hope not," answered Hardy. "Yes," replied Nelson, "my backbone is shot through." He was carried below; but, though from the first the wound was recognised as mortal, he did not die for more than three hours. His fall was speedily avenged; for though it was not known who fired the fatal shot, not a man came out of the *Redoutable's* mizen-top alive.

The French musketry, however, was at this time very deadly. Within a few minutes after Nelson's fall, several other officers of the *Victory* and about forty men were killed or wounded, and her upper deck was so far cleared that Captain Lucas of the *Redoutable* again thought that a determined effort to board might be successful. But both ships, and more especially the *Victory*, tumbled home so much, that, while at the water-line they were grinding against each other, at the upper deck they were many feet apart, and to pass from one to the other was no easy matter. A few men did, indeed, scramble on to the *Victory's* quarter-deck, but were at once repulsed, though the doing so again exposed the *Victory's* people to the deadly French musketry, and several of them, including Captain Adair of the marines, were shot down. Lucas had meantime lowered the main-yard to serve as a bridge, and his men were swarming on the quarter-deck and forecastle, waiting for the moment to cross over, when the *Téméraire*, coming under her starboard quarter, swept them away with a terrible raking broadside, which, it is said, killed or wounded upwards of two hundred men. The effect was decisive; all power of resistance was beaten out of her, and when the *Téméraire* ran on board her on the starboard side, she struck her flag and was quietly taken possession of. Her loss in killed and wounded was returned as five hundred and twenty-two out of a complement of six hundred and forty-three.

The *Redoutable* was scarcely secured, and the *Victory* was still in the act of disengaging herself from her, when the *Fougueux*, which had been already very roughly handled by the *Royal Sovereign* and the leading ships of the lee division, appeared through the smoke on the *Téméraire's* starboard quarter. When within a few yards distant, she received the *Téméraire's* starboard broadside double-shotted. Not a gun could miss its mark. In the smoke and confusion she fell on board the *Téméraire*, and was immediately lashed by her fore-rigging to the *Téméraire's* spare anchor. A small party of men under the first-lieutenant, Mr. Kennedy, sprang on board; the feeble resistance was at once overpowered, and her flag was hauled down a few minutes before two o'clock; she is said to have had more than four hundred men killed or wounded.

The *Victory* had meanwhile cleared herself from the group, and was standing towards the north as well as her crippled state would permit. The *Téméraire* lay for a considerable time entangled between the two prizes, and with the wreck of the *Redoutable's* mizen-mast across her quarter-deck; but, except in firing an occasional gun at long range, there was no further fighting for either *Victory* or *Téméraire.* For, in fact, the battle was by this time practically over.

It is impossible to describe the action of each ship in detail. The smoke and the confusion of lines were so great that even at the time individual ships had not always a very clear idea of what ships they were engaged with, and still less of what other ships were doing. The various accounts which have come down to us are thus extremely confused or even contradictory; and the attempt to disentangle them can lead to no quite satisfactory result. It is enough to say that, once the heads of the English columns were well engaged, the other ships made no pretence of keeping their line, further than they were compelled by the faintness of the breeze and by their rate of sailing. Each made the best of her way towards the enemy's line, and fell on such of the enemy's ships as she happened to meet with. But the dominating plan given out by Nelson, and now carried into effect by Collingwood and himself, ensured the English being present on the immediate scene of action in superior force. The number of ships of the line in the allied fleet was thirty-three; but the ten in the van were virtually excluded from the fight, and the other twenty-three were brought into it only by degrees as the English ships came up.

There is no doubt that, under any conditions of weather, and more especially in the very light breeze which actually prevailed, the advance of the English columns would have been extremely dangerous had the enemy had more efficient gunners. But the low state of gunnery in both French and Spanish navies was perfectly well known to Nelson, and was an important item in his calculation; otherwise he would scarcely have placed the *Royal Sovereign* and *Victory* in positions where they must be knocked to pieces without the chance of firing a shot. Even as it was, it will be seen in the table on pages 218-19 how severe was the loss of the two headmost ships in each column in comparison with that of the other ships. The number of killed and wounded in these four, the *Victory* and *Téméraire*, *Royal Sovereign* and *Belleisle*, together with that in the *Bellerophon* and *Colossus*, the fifth and sixth ships in the lee line, was considerably more than the half of that in the whole fleet. But, this danger once passed, the advantage was wholly with the English, who could and did oppose two or three or four ships to one of the enemy, sometimes at once, sometimes in rapid succession, till that one and the rest, one by one, yielded to overpowering numbers. And thus, within two hours from the time the *Royal Sovereign* fired her broadside into the stern of the *Santa Ana*, the victory was assured.

The *Santa Ana*, raked in succession by the *Belleisle* and other ships as they passed in, closely engaged the whole time by the *Royal Sovereign*, having lost all her masts and with half her men killed or wounded, struck her flag about a quarter-past two. Vice-Admiral Alava was himself severely wounded, and was allowed to remain on board the *Santa Ana*. Other ships, French and Spanish, were similarly overpowered by numbers. The *Monarca, Bahama, Algésiras, Swiftsure, Berwick,* and many others, were terribly beaten, and lost some three or four hundred men each before they struck their colours. But the odds were everywhere against them. Here, out of many, are two instances. The *Bucentaure*,

after the first terrible broadside from the *Victory*
which virtually sealed her fate, was successively
engaged by the *Neptune, Leviathan,* and *Conqueror,* to
which last she struck her colours.   Captain Atcherley,
of the marines, with five men, was sent in a boat to take
possession ; and to him, on the *Bucentaure's* quarter-deck,
the French Commander - in - Chief and his staff offered
their swords.   Atcherley, however, considered it unbecoming for him to receive the submission of an officer
of Villeneuve's rank, and took him, with the first and
second captains, in his boat to return to the *Conqueror.*
But the *Conqueror* had made sail in search of a fresh
antagonist, and the illustrious prisoners were taken on
board the *Mars,* where they remained.   The *Neptune,*
followed by the *Leviathan* and afterwards by the *Conqueror,*
had meanwhile engaged the *Santisima Trinidad,* which
had already suffered severely from the more distant port
broadside of the *Victory.*   At about half-past two she
was completely dismasted, and took no further part in
the fight, but was not actually taken possession of till
three hours later.

All this time the ships in the allied van made no
movement to support their centre and rear.   It was
not till two o'clock and after Villeneuve had repeatedly
signalled to them, that they began to wear.   But the
breeze had been gradually dying away, while the swell
from the west was still very heavy.   It took the ships
nearly an hour to get round on to the starboard tack.
Some of them were towed round by their boats ; the
Intrépide fouled the *Mont-Blanc,* and lost her foremast.
And when they were at last round, Dumanoir in the
Formidable, with four of the others, held a close luff aud

stood to windward of the field of battle, while the other
five kept away to leeward. Three of them passed to
the south-east and joined Gravina. The *San Augustino,*
less fortunate, was brought to close action by the
Leviathan, which, after delivering one treble-shotted
broadside at less than fifty yards distance, fell on board
her and took possession without further resistance.
About the same time the *Intrépide* was brought to
action by the little *Africa,* and detained till the *Orion*
came up. A quarter of an hour later her main and mizen
masts went over the side ; she had lost two hundred men,
killed or wounded. The *Ajax* and *Agamemnon* were both
drawing near, and she struck her colours. It was then
some little time after five o'clock.

Meanwhile, Dumanoir with the other five ships was
endeavouring to pass clear to windward. If all the ten
ships of the van had kept with him, it is possible that he
might have brought them in compact order against the
scattered English; and though it cannot be supposed that
he could have retrieved the fortune of the day, he might
have caused the English some serious loss, and at any
rate have enabled some of the beaten ships to effect
their escape. When, however, he found himself with
only five, his heart failed him : he judged that to plunge
into the fight with these would be but to sacrifice them
also ; and so, interchanging a distant and desultory fire
with some of the English ships, he passed away towards
the south-west and made good his escape with the four
French ships. The fifth, the Spanish *Neptuno,* whether
less weatherly than her consorts, whether through the
unwillingness of her captain to withdraw from the battle
before it was definitely lost, or through his want of

decision, fell considerably to leeward, and was brought to action by the *Minotaur* and *Spartiate*, which, being the rearmost ships of the weather line, had not got into action when Dumanoir's movement gave them the chance. They had hauled to the wind on the port tack, but were already too far to leeward to intercept the retreat of the *Formidable* and the other French ships. They were, however, able to engage the *Neptuno*, which, after a gallant defence, struck her flag a little after five o'clock. It seems doubtful whether she or the *Intrépide* was the last to surrender.

This was the end of the battle. Eighteen of the enemy's ships had been captured and the rest had fled. Gravina, whose ship, the *Principe de Asturias*, was terribly shattered, and who was himself mortally wounded, hoisted the signal to rally, and made sail to the north-ward. Ten other ships gathered round, and with him made good their escape for the time. They were not pursued, for Nelson was no more. After three hours of intense pain and partial unconsciousness, he expired about half-past four, with the ejaculation, "Thank God! I have done my duty."

One incident of the battle still remains to be told. The French *Achille* had suffered severely in successive engagements with her English namesake, the *Belleisle*, *Swiftsure*, and *Polyphemus*. She had lost her mizen-mast, main-topmast and foreyard; and when, owing, it was supposed, to her swivels or musketry, she caught fire in the fore-top, it was found that her fire-engine had been destroyed and that she was without the means of extinguishing the flames. About half-past four, while her crew were trying to cut away the mast so that it

might fall clear, a broadside from the *Prince*, just coming
into action, shot it away half-way up, so that the flam-
ing top fell into the waist and set fire to the boats and
to the ship herself.   The *Prince* fired one or two more
broadsides before the helpless state of the *Achille* became
evident.   She then wore round, hove to, and sent her
boats to endeavour to save the lives of the men.   The
Swiftsure did the same.   It was a service of no little
danger, for the *Achille's* guns were loaded and went off
as the flames reached them.   Some two hundred of her
men had been rescued when, about a quarter to six, the
fire reached her magazine and she blew up, with the loss
of all still surviving.   It appears doubtful whether she had
actually struck her flag or not ; and some French writers
have prided themselves on the alleged fact of her going
down with colours flying.   If she did, it was the result
of forgetfulness or preoccupation on both sides, and not
of any desperate determination on the part of either the
officers or men of the *Achille*.   All effort at defence had
unquestionably ceased before the *Prince* sent a boat to
her assistance.

About noon, and before the first shot was fired,
Nelson had made the general signal, "Prepare to anchor
immediately after the close of day."   He knew, of course,
that many of the ships would be dismasted or crippled :
he had no doubt whatever that many of the enemy's
ships, in a similar condition, would be in our hands ;
and a falling barometer seemed to portend bad weather.
After he was carried below, the necessity of anchoring
was continually present to his mind, and he repeatedly
urged it on Hardy, desiring him to see that it was done.
When, however, immediately after the firing ceased,

Hardy went on board the *Royal Sovereign* and acquainted Collingwood with Nelson's death and last wishes, Collingwood exclaimed, "Anchor the fleet! that is the last thing I should have thought of"; and, as the command now devolved on him, he did not anchor. The ships were by this time in thirteen fathoms water, and the westerly swell was setting them slowly towards the shoals of Trafalgar, now only a few miles distant. The wind was gradually freshening, and at the same time backing. By midnight it was blowing hard from about south-south-west, and the ships' heads were laid off shore; but the dismasted and shattered prizes, with only a handful of men on board to navigate them, were at the mercy of the weather, or of the prisoners, who had to be released in order that they might not be drowned like mice in a cage. One of the prizes was thus retaken; others, having drifted near Cadiz, were retaken by a bold sortie of the enemy, who, however, lost more than they gained; some were wrecked; many were scuttled and sunk to avoid greater risk; and thus it happened that of all the ships captured on the 21st, four only were taken to Gibraltar as trophies of the victory, and these by a cruel chance were all old and worthless.

The effective trophies were supplied by Dumanoir's four ships which escaped to the south-west. After making a good offing, they turned to the north, hoping to reach Brest or one of the ports in the bay. They had all sustained some damage, which, though not serious, was more than might have been supposed, considering the very partial way in which they had been engaged. Their masts were more or less wounded, and they were making water at such a rate as to need to keep the pumps going. The *Formidable* had been obliged to throw twelve of her guns overboard : three others had been dismounted at Trafalgar. Off Cape Ortegal, on November 4th, they fell in with a squadron of four ships of the line and four heavy frigates under the command of Sir Richard Strachan in the *Cæsar*, and were captured without much difficulty. They were all added to the English navy ; one of them, the *Duguay-Trouin*, whose name was changed to *Implacable*, is still afloat at Devonport, where she is used as a training-ship for boys.

From the purely naval point of view, then, the result of the Battle of Trafalgar may be stated thus.

SHIPS OF THE LINE OF BATTLE.

PRESENT IN THE ACTION.		
French.	Spanish.	Total.
18	15	33

HOW DISPOSED OF.	French.	Spanish.	Total.
Captured on 21st	9	9	...
Recaptured on 22nd	1	...	...
Recaptured on 23rd	...	2	...
Leaving prizes	8	7	15
Captured on 24th	...	1	1
Wrecked on 24th	1	1	2
Captured on Nov. 4th	4	...	4
In Cadiz	5	6	11
			33

Those in Cadiz were all much shattered, quite unfit for service, and were never at sea again as ships of war.

The Battle of Trafalgar thus completely broke up the
threatening coalition of France and Spain which Bonaparte had formed against us.   Any further prosecution
of his scheme for the invasion of England was rendered
impossible, and was, in fact, never again thought of.
The naval power of France was, for the time, completely
broken; and during the rest of the war, which lasted
for another ten years, the command of the sea was held
by us in a grip which the enemy scarcely attempted to
dispute.   That is the historical importance of the battle;
but of almost greater importance are the lessons it conveys to the modern successors of those who so nobly
fought and conquered ninety years ago.   There is a
widespread notion that, grand as was this masterpiece
of our greatest sailor, the times, and with them the
art of navigation and of naval war, have so changed, that
we may admire but cannot find anything to imitate.
This would seem to spring out of some idea that the
principles of war depend on the accidents of the age
rather than on the immutable laws of nature.   But so
long as seas roll and men live, so long will skill, temper,
and courage control the mere accessories of ships and
guns, of sails or engines.

The rest may be told in very few words.   Collingwood's despatches reached the Admiralty early on the
morning of November 6th, and the Park and Tower
guns announced the victory to the public; but as the
story was read in the *Gazette* on the same day, the
splendour of the achievement was almost forgotten
in grief for the loss which England had sustained.
Such honours and rewards as the Crown and a grateful
country could bestow were freely given to the hero's

family.   On November 9th his brother William was
gazetted as Earl Nelson of Trafalgar, with remainder to
the heirs-male successively of his sisters Mrs. Bolton
and Mrs. Matcham; and in the course of the following
session the House of Commons liberally endowed the
title, gave £15,000 to each of the sisters, and £2000 a
year for life to Lady Nelson; and to her, as well as to
the Earl as an heirloom, the Patriotic Fund voted a
vase of the value of £500.   It was noticed at the time,
and has often been commented on since, that no attention was paid to the so-called codicil in favour of Lady
Hamilton.   It has been maintained that it was the duty
of the country to provide for her, not only as the woman
whom he addressed as his dear wife in the sight of
Heaven, but also as the woman who had rendered great
and important services to the State.   But the Government knew, what has been made public only within the
last few years, that Nelson was entirely deceived as to
Lady Hamilton's alleged services, which existed, indeed,
only in her own imagination; they knew also that she
was left well provided for both by her husband's will
and by Nelson's.   They may reasonably have thought
that £2000 a year was a sufficient income for such a
woman.   She, however, speedily ran through it, was
imprisoned for debt, was released by private charity,
and during her last years was dependent on the interest
of the £4000 settled on her daughter Horatia.   She
resided in Calais, in humble cirumstances but by no
means in absolute want; became a Roman Catholic,—
possibly a sincere one; and dying at Calais in 1815,
was buried there in accordance with the rites of the
Catholic Church.

The *Victory*, with Nelson's body on board, arrived at Spithead on December 5th, and was sent round to the Thames. The body was then taken to Greenwich Hospital, where, in the Painted Hall, it lay in state from January 4th to the 8th, to be visited and wept over by thousands. On the 8th it was conveyed in a solemn procession of boats to Whitehall Stairs; thence on foot to the Admiralty; and the next day to St. Paul's, where it was placed in the crypt, in a sarcophagus made at the cost of Cardinal Wolsey for Henry the Eighth. Above, in the cathedral, is a monument by Flaxman. Other monuments were erected by scores through the country; scarcely a town of any size but has one. But the truest, the noblest, the grandest monument is in the hearts of the English people, where, purified from all earthly taint, his memory lives enshrined as the ideal of heroism, of self-sacrifice, and of duty.

THE END

English Men of Action Series.

Crown 8vo. Cloth. With Portraits. 2s. 6d. each.

CAMPBELL (COLIN).
By A. FORBES.

CLIVE.
By Colonel Sir CHARLES WILSON.

COOK (CAPTAIN).
By WALTER BESANT.

DAMPIER.
By W. CLARK RUSSELL.

DRAKE.
By JULIAN CORBETT.

DUNDONALD.
By Hon. J. W. FORTESCUE.

GORDON (GENERAL).
By Colonel Sir W. BUTLER.

HASTINGS (WARREN).
By Sir A. LYALL.

HAVELOCK (SIR HENRY).
By A. FORBES.

HENRY V.
By Rev. A. J. CHURCH.

LAWRENCE (LORD).
By Sir RICHARD TEMPLE.

LIVINGSTONE.
By THOMAS HUGHES.

MONK.
By JULIAN CORBETT.

MONTROSE.
By MOWBRAY MORRIS.

NAPIER (SIR CHARLES).
By Sir W. BUTLER.

NELSON.
By J. K. LAUGHTON.

PETERBOROUGH.
By W. STEBBING.

RODNEY.
By DAVID HANNAY.

STRAFFORD.
By H. D. TRAILL.

WARWICK, the King-maker.
By C. W. OMAN.

WELLINGTON.
By GEORGE HOOPER.

WOLFE.
By A. G. BRADLEY.

TWELVE ENGLISH STATESMEN.

Crown 8vo. 2s. 6d. each.

* *A Series of Short Biographies, not designed to be a complete roll of famou* *Statesmen, but to present in historic order the lives and work of those leading actors i* *our affairs who by their direct influence have left an abiding mark on the policy, th* *institutions, and the position of Great Britain among States.*

WILLIAM THE CON-QUEROR. By EDWARD A. FREEMAN, D.C.L., LL.D., late Regius Professor of Modern History in the University of Oxford.

HENRY II.
By Mrs. J. R. GREEN.

EDWARD I.
By T. F. TOUT, M.A., Owens College, Manchester.

HENRY VII.
By JAMES GAIRDNER.

CARDINAL WOLSEY.
By Bishop CREIGHTON, D.D., late Dixie Professor of Ecclesiastical History in the University of Cambridge.

ELIZABETH.
By E. S. BEESLY, M.A., Professor o Modern History, University College London.

OLIVER CROMWELL.
By FREDERIC HARRISON.

WILLIAM III.
By H. D. TRAILL.

WALPOLE.
By JOHN MORLEY.

CHATHAM.
By JOHN MORLEY. [*In preparation*

PITT.
By Lord ROSEBERY.

PEEL.
By J. R. THURSFIELD, M.A., late Fellow of Jesus College, Oxford.

MACMILLAN AND CO., LONDON.